All the Wisdom in One Place

By
Shawn D. Williamson

All the Wisdom in One Place

Copyright © 2025

Shawn D. Williamson

Serious Publishing Corp
6240 S. Lindbergh, Ste 101
St. Louis, MO 63123
314-845-7999

ISBN 979-8-218-62011-0

Printed in the United States of America.

TABLE OF CONTENTS

Introduction

"If you would not be forgotten as soon as you are dead and rotten, either write something worth reading or do things worth the writing." – Benjamin Franklin

I begin this book with a quote from my favorite American. I would argue that there never was and may never be an American more dedicated to disseminating wisdom to the people than Benjamin Franklin. He spent over 25 years writing, printing, and distributing Poor Richard's Almanack (yes, I spelled it correctly) to the colonists between 1732 and 1758. It was full of common sayings, aphorisms, and proverbs that were useful in the everyday lives of the brave, independent people who founded this country. Many of the sayings are still repeated today in nearly every household in America. His almanacs were full of wisdom, and that is the point of this book: to spread the wisdom of the wise.

Franklin is long dead, but he is not forgotten. I have taken up the cause to disseminate wisdom to you, wisdom that can help us all think and live better, prosper, and find happiness and meaning in life.

Why am I so interested in wisdom? I view it as one of the fundamental purposes of my life. Everyone should have a purpose, whether that is to cure cancer, teach children to read, bring food to the hungry, bring water to the thirsty, create timeless art, or accomplish one of a million other important goals.

Allow me to address the book title issue. Some will say, "Clearly this is not ALL of the wisdom that exists." That is indeed true. However, *All of the Wisdom I Can Fit into a Book Short Enough to Read* just seemed too unwieldy.

The format of this book is to quote verbatim for you the wisdom that I have read, heard, seen in action, and found to be true during the course of my fifty-plus years on the planet. You should always consider the source when anyone tries to teach you anything, so if you would like to read a brief description about this wisdom compiler (me), you can do that in the "About the Author" section at the end of this book.

The order of wisdom here is simply alphabetical by the most commonly used name of the author. Some of the quotes don't need much discussion or explanation, but in most cases I give my opinion on what the quote means, why it's important, or how it relates to our lives today. You certainly may not need or want my interpretation, and that is totally fine. However, what is obvious to you is not always obvious to everyone. Some wisdom is a bit below the surface, and you have to dig a little to see it clearly. If you disagree with my interpretations or assessments, that's fine, too. You might jot down your own thoughts next to the quote. The important thing here is that you think about the words and wisdom, grow, and become wiser in the process.

Before we go seeking wisdom together, let's define it so that we both understand what we're looking for. The Merriam-Webster Dictionary defines wisdom like this: "the ability to discern inner qualities and relationships, insight, good sense, judgement, a generally accepted belief, accumulated philosophical or scientific learning, or the teachings of the ancient wise men." Kind of vague, right? Here is my take on it.... Wisdom is discernment or judgement that comes from real experience and leads to better decisions and outcomes.

My goal with this book is to have you finish it and say to yourself, "I've learned some valuable concepts here that I need to put into practice." I would like you to feel that the time and dollars you spent were worth the investment. If you think there is indeed valuable wisdom within, please share this book with others, or buy them their own copy. Wisdom is one of the best things you can pass along to those you care about. Onward.....

All the Wisdom in One Place

John Adams
Co-author of the Declaration of Independence and the
Massachusetts Constitution. First Vice-President and second
President of the United States. 1735 to 1826

**"Posterity! You will never know how much it cost the
present generation to preserve your freedom! I hope you
will make a good use of it."**

> We can read ad infinitum about the American Revolution,
> but it is impossible to understand what the founding fathers
> risked and the price they paid to take on the most powerful
> army in the world and win our independence nearly 250
> years ago. We owe it to their memory to maintain that
> freedom in perpetuity and "make good use of it."

Charles Addams
American cartoonist and creator of the fictional character
Morticia Addams of the Addams Family comics, TV series, and
films. 1912 to 1988

**"Normal is an illusion. What is normal for the spider is
chaos for the fly."**

> Have you ever thought about this idea of what is considered
> "normal"? Should you worry about whether people
> consider your behavior normal? Growing up, I thought
> about it a lot. My conclusion was that if you accept the
> premise that no two humans are exactly alike, then it seems
> there can be only one person whose behavior is perfectly
> normal.

Maya Angelou
American writer, poet, and civil rights activist. 1928 to 2014

**"At the end of the day, people won't remember what you
said or did, they will remember how you made them feel."**

> I have met a small number of people during my life who
> attempt to bully everyone they meet - taking whatever they
> want and trying to raise themselves up by diminishing
> everyone around them. It's a bad way to be, and most of

them have gotten their just rewards eventually. I can name every one of those folks, and so can the people they've trampled. You and I need to strive towards the other end of that spectrum. We need to aspire to be the people who lift up those around us and make other people feel good about themselves. We should build up our friends, family, coworkers, and community and strive to be remembered for the good feelings we brought to them.

Susan B. Anthony
Major American women's rights activist and champion for a woman's right to vote. 1820 to 1906

"We throw to the winds the old dogma that governments can give rights. Before governments were organized, no one denies that each individual possessed the right to protect his own life, liberty, and property."

It sounds like Anthony subscribed to the founding fathers' ideas that there are certain unalienable rights that we are all born with, such as life, liberty, and the pursuit of happiness. It should never be that governments grant us rights, but rather, we the people grant certain citizens among us the temporary power to govern.

"Independence is happiness."

Several studies indicate that autonomy is one of the key components of job satisfaction. If we are free and independent, at least we have the opportunity to pursue our own dreams, goals, and activities that may make us happy.

Thomas Aquinas
Italian priest, philosopher, and theologian. Some say he was the most influential thinker of the medieval era. 1225 to 1274

"There is nothing on this earth more to be prized than true friendship."

Envision that you had more money, houses, cars, boats, and planes than anyone on earth but not one friend to share those treasures and experiences with. All of it would be for naught. Now envision that your possessions were close to nil, but you spent every day hiking around the forest and mountains, swimming at the beach, and talking around the campfire with 15 incredible, devoted friends – a pretty happy life indeed. Hence, the value of a true friendship becomes virtually incalculable, and a life without friends is pretty poor, regardless of your monetary wealth.

"Better to illuminate than merely to shine, to deliver to others contemplated truths than merely to contemplate."

Contemplation is for your benefit in this one lifetime, but sharing truth with others can benefit countless numbers in multiple lifetimes. That is one of my goals with this book – to try to add just a little illumination to the world that can be shared and can float on into the future.

Aristotle
One of the top ancient Greek intellectuals who lived from 384 to 322 BC. He was a writer, philosopher, and teacher who covered many subjects including physics, metaphysics, logic, ethics, poetry, music, psychology, language, economics, government, meteorology, geology, biology, and zoology.

"Knowing yourself is the beginning of all wisdom."

Unfortunately, it takes some of us 30 or 40 years to truly understand ourselves, but it's an important step towards finding the right place for yourself in the world. A lot of people spend little time thinking about where they are supposed to be and what they are supposed to be doing. That is unfortunate because I believe it is only when you are in the right place doing the right thing that real success, happiness, and fulfillment is realized.

"He who has overcome his fears will truly be free."

So many people live in irrational fear of imagined dangers. It holds them back from achieving their highest potential and purpose.

"The high-minded man must care more for the truth than for what people think."

We need more truth today and less concern about optics or society's rules for political correctness. Over the years I have watched many young people (and some old ones) restrain themselves from what they really want to say or do for fear of someone's judgement – normally judgement that doesn't matter.

"We are what we repeatedly do; excellence, then, is not an act but a habit."

The idea of becoming what you do is kind of hard to accept, but think about someone who has been a teacher or a pastor for 30 years. Has it changed them? Of course. In many ways, they become what they do. The people who are excellent at something probably do it every day and continuously strive for improvement. Acting out excellence repeatedly eventually turns into true excellence.

"Dignity does not consist in possessing honors, but in deserving them."

So true in the social media internet age. How many people today in the entertainment, sports, and political realms possess honors without deserving them? And, how many non-famous people, who quietly deserve honors, are not getting them? We should fix this situation to the extent that we can. Notice when the people around you deserve honors, and deliver those honors even if they are only from you and you alone. A couple of months ago, I met a grandpa in his 60's in the park. He was raising his two grandchildren (ages 4 and 7) because his drug-addicted daughter was permanently roaming about out-of-state. After hearing his story, I said, "On behalf of the universe,

thank you for being a good man and raising these children."
It's not much, but he'll remember for a little while that
someone noticed his sacrifice and honored him.

**"The aim of art is to represent not the outward appearance
of things, but their inward significance."**

In other words, there should be more to art than meets the
eye. Great art goes beyond the paint on the canvas. It
harbors a deeper meaning, and it is that deeper meaning
that makes the art compelling and extraordinary.

**"We give up leisure in order that we may have leisure, just
as we go to war in order that we may have peace."**

Those are a couple of real paradoxes. How do you gain
leisure through labor and gain peace through war? Many
are laboring more now in order to have more leisure later in
retirement. The theory is sound, but some folks never
make it to the leisure phase of life due to bad luck or
neglected health, which is tragic. Similarly, some wars
unfortunately do not end in the peace that is visualized by
the war-makers. Some wars end in peace because there is
no one left to fight. I feel that we need to regularly re-
assess whether the warpaths we are on are leading us
towards peace or just unending wars.

Isaac Asimov
American science fiction author and professor of biochemistry
at Boston University. 1920 to 1992

**"The saddest aspect of life right now is that science gathers
knowledge faster than society gathers wisdom."**

This was written long before the internet began. How
much more true is it today? I have had the notion for at
least twenty years that society is gaining technology much
faster than it is gaining civility. You could also say that we
are gaining weapons (of all sorts) faster than we are gaining
the judgement for when and how to use them. It's a scary
trajectory for humanity.

<u>Lee Atwater</u>
American political consultant and advisor to presidents Ronald
Reagan and George H. W. Bush. 1951 to 1991

"Perception is reality."

> It is very important to understand this concept, and I have
> heard several people question the meaning of the phrase.
> They'll say, "That's ridiculous; reality is reality." True.
> Yet, our perception of a situation may or may not be
> reality. I think the saying could be more accurately stated
> as "perception might as well be reality" because however
> someone perceives a situation is how they are going to
> respond to it. Hence, when you are doing something
> important, try hard to think about not just what you are
> doing but also how your actions are being perceived. This
> is why texting and emailing scares me a little bit. You
> cannot see body language or hear the tone of voice. When
> you have something dicey to discuss, try to do it via phone
> call, video conference, or ideally in person.

<u>St. Augustine of Hippo</u>
Ancient author, theologian, and philosopher from Roman North
Africa. He was an important priest and bishop in the early
Catholic church. 354 to 430 AD

**"The world is a book, and those who do not travel read only
a page."**

> Even when it was so difficult to travel, some early
> philosophers, such as St. Augustine, recognized the
> enormous expansion of perspective you can achieve by way
> of travel abroad. Only when you experience the ancient
> monuments and immerse yourself in the local culture do
> you begin to understand a place.

**"Resentment is like drinking poison and waiting for the
other person to die."**

> When I first heard this quote, it struck a chord in me. It's
> easy to hang on to anger and bitterness for the wrongs

you've endured. It's easy to hate people for years for the pain they have caused you, but the reality is that they are out there living their own lives, not worrying at all about your anger, bitterness, and thoughts of revenge. So, either get on with the revenge, or get over the resentment. Otherwise, you are just wasting a bunch of your time and energy drinking poison and waiting for the other person to die.

"It seems to me that an unjust law is no law at all."

Laws are meant to promote fairness, justice, and civility within society, and they are meant to be obeyed. When a law does not seem fair, just, or right, the people will tend to ignore it. Even those tasked with enforcing the unjust law may ignore it, as well.

Marcus Aurelius
Roman emperor of the second century and stoic philosopher. He took extensive notes aimed at self-improvement while he was emperor, 161 to 180 AD Those notes were later organized into a collection called *Meditations*. 121 to 180 AD

"Our life is what our thoughts make it."

Many of the great philosophers and teachers have come to this same conclusion. Whatever you keep thinking about becomes what you are talking about, then what you are doing, and eventually who you are. Hence, to the extent possible, control your thoughts, and steer them in a positive direction.

"Do not act as if you had ten thousand years to throw away. Death stands at your elbow. Be good for something while you live and it is in your power."

It's easy to feel like you're immortal at 18, maybe even all the way to 35, but at some point you start realizing how short a lifetime is. Some high school classmates, relatives, good friends, and perhaps even your parents may be gone.

We aren't promised any particular number of years, so we need to feel the urgency to get to work, serving our purpose and doing what we are supposed to do in this life.

"Natural ability without education has more often raised a man to glory and virtue than education without natural ability."

It's true that natural ability can exceed education. Look at the billionaires who dropped out of college. Don't get me wrong; college can be a key to open a path for people to pursue their natural abilities. It can be of great use, but it certainly doesn't guarantee success. I like to say that those with natural born charisma can hardly fail, and those devoid of charisma can hardly succeed. Charisma may or may not be amongst your natural abilities. If it is, great. If it is not, then I recommend educating yourself on what it is and how you can improve it.

"When you arise in the morning, think of what a precious privilege it is to be alive – to breathe, to think, to enjoy, to love."

You will occasionally hear gratitude for being alive, but it's pretty rare. I aspire to feel more gratitude more often for this incredible gift that you and I have been given. We are breathing and thinking and have the chance to find joy and love every day. There have been over 100 billion people on earth who can't do those things anymore.

Averroes
Actually named Ibn Rushd, he was an Andalusian polymath and well-known author of over a hundred books. 1126 to 1198

"Ignorance leads to fear, fear leads to hate, and hate leads to violence. This is the equation."

Over 800 years later, we are still seeing this equation play out during the so-called "information age." Ironically, for eons ignorance was the result of the lack of printed material and the slow speed of communication. Now, ignorance (and confusion) stems from the overload of printed materials and lightning speed of communication.

"An army of philosophers would not be sufficient to change the nature of error and to make it truth."

Likewise, an army of propaganda purveyors today still cannot change lies into truth. Do not let any group, no matter their numbers, convince you something is true that you know to be false, based on your own observation, logic, and reason.

Sai Baba
Indian spiritual master of the late 19th century, revered by both Hindu and Muslim followers. 1926 to 2011

"Life is a song – sing it. Life is a game – play it. Life is a challenge – meet it. Life is a dream – realize it. Life is a sacrifice – offer it. Life is love – enjoy it.

What a beautiful summation of the meaning of life. Go make the most of what life has to offer.

Francis Bacon
English Viscount and Chancellor in the 16th and 17th centuries, who promoted the scientific method, which entails testing hypothesis via experimentation and observation. 1561 to 1626

"He that gives good advice, builds with one hand. He that gives good counsel and example, builds with both."

When I ran an accounting firm, I always kept in mind that I needed to not only clearly define what I wanted from employees but also to model it. Most people are not going to work harder than the boss does. It's human nature. If they are asked to do more than their supervisor, it's going to build unproductive resentment. This same idea could be applied to parenting. Would you expect a child to behave better than his parents? Not likely. We need to give good advice, and be a good example.

David Ben-Gurion
One of the most important founders of the modern state of
Israel and its first prime minister. 1886 to 1973

**"Without moral and intellectual independence, there is no
anchor for national independence.**

We must have the freedom to live as we want and think as
we like. If we cannot do that in whatever country we live
in, then we will not care much to defend that country's
sovereignty from whatever forces try to destroy it.

Yogi Berra
Lawrence Peter "Yogi" Berra was an American baseball player,
manager, and coach. 1925 to 2015

"It ain't over 'til it's over."

This statement seems like there isn't much to it, but there
certainly is. He was reminding us that as long as the game
is in play, anything can happen. Don't give up and concede
until it's really over. A couple years ago I was playing
chess against my daughter's boyfriend. I made a mistake
and eventually found myself with just two pawns against
his queen. I seemingly had no chance, but I carried on.
After a few moves, when putting me into check, he
cavalierly and accidentally moved his queen adjacent to
one of my pawns and then lost it. And, shortly thereafter,
he lost the game. I'm sure you can think of dozens of
come-from-behind victories and last-second wins that
you've seen or participated in. Never give up!

"You can observe a lot by just watching."

This reminds me of the quote by Epictetus about listening
twice as much as you speak. I think Yogi's point is that
most of us don't spend enough time just observing a
situation in order to learn how something works. He was
probably watching how pitchers throw or how batters
swing, but this advice could be helpful for almost any

acquired skill: carpentry, sculpting, plumbing, brick-laying, surgery, welding, and many others.

"It's déjà vu all over again."

This is another funny quote. Envision watching your team lose for the same reason it lost last time. It's important to notice trends in life. It's especially helpful if you can notice mistakes that you tend to repeat. For instance, every time you skip studying for a test, you fail the test. So, when something starts to feel like negative déjà vu all over again, nip that bad sequence of events in the bud, if possible. Learn from your mistakes; don't repeat them.

"When you come to a fork in the road, take it."

This one sounds silly, but it's actually accurate, important, and has two meanings. In the literal sense, if you find something free and useful (like a fork) along your journey, pick it up and keep it. In the figurative sense, when you come to a split in the road with a path to the left and a path to the right, pick one and keep moving. Too many people get stuck for too long at the fork in the road. Some call it "analysis paralysis," and it can lead to losing the opportunities down both potential paths. So, consider everything you know about the two paths you face. Do your homework, and consult with wise men and women. Then, pick a path, and make the very best of it with haste.

Ambrose Bierce
American satirical short-story writer, poet, and journalist, who was also a long-serving civil war veteran. 1842 to 1914

"Before undergoing a surgical procedure, arrange your temporal affairs. You may live."

I love this quote. It's funny and points out the absurdity of the way some people procrastinate. They come to the realization, "Oh, I'm about to have a risky surgery; I better put my affairs in order." Really? Any of us may have a car accident tomorrow. Doesn't that reality suggest that we should already have our "affairs in order"? Why not take care of business when there is not a life-threatening deadline at hand? I will end this soap-box rant with the old adage, why put off until tomorrow what you can do today?

"Lawsuit: A machine which you go into as a pig and come out of as a sausage."

I'm not a fan of litigation. I have observed too many cases where both sides lose, and their attorneys win. One's quest to even the score can result in attorney fees that surpass the successful collection of damages. Also, always keep in mind that no matter how hard you squeeze, you can't get blood from a turnip. (This means people who are broke can't give you any money, even if they are legally required to do so.)

Josh Billings
Josh Billings was the pen name of Henry Wheeler Shaw. He was a 19th century American author and humorist, a contemporary of Mark Twain. 1818 to 1885

"Common sense is the knack of seeing things as they are and doing things as they ought to be done."

This is what I want from mayors, governors, senators, and presidents. Using common sense is how you find real solutions to real problems. Unfortunately, as Voltaire said, "Common sense is not so common."

"Life consists not in holding good cards but in playing those you hold well."

True. The first hand we are dealt is out of our control. It is up to us to take it from there, and play the best we can with all of the subsequent cards.

"There are lots of people who mistake their imagination for their memory."

This sounds like Billings is talking about politicians. The important point here is that sometimes people are telling you a falsehood because they don't remember it accurately. It does not even have to be intentional fabrication, but bad information is bad information. Don't put all of your faith into, or bet your life on, someone else's memory. You might even want to document important information in your own life to protect you from your own memory.

"Be like a postage stamp. Stick to one thing until you get there."

I love this simile. It's a simple instruction that is powerful if you can follow it. Look at the most highly paid and highly acclaimed people in the world. Most of them do one thing, and they do it very well. I've delivered this one-thing message to a few of my friends over the years, friends who are like myself. By nature, they try to run in multiple directions at the same time or get bored easily and keep rotating their attention to new projects. One of these friends recently told me what he thought about my theory of sticking to one thing at a time. He said, "I hate it, but you're right about that."

"There is no revenge so complete as forgiveness."

I don't know if I would call it revenge or resolution. Either way, it is an excellent way to resolve a vendetta. My guess is that Billings was thinking, "Hey, you know that bad thing you did to me? I don't care about that anymore. I'm not going to dwell on it or even think about it. I forgive you." This idea is very important to absorb: spending days, months, and years being angry at someone just wastes a lot of your time and energy, while the target of your anger is not thinking about you at all.

George Caleb Bingham
Missouri politician, soldier, and artist. 1811 to 1879

"Many are always praising the by-gone time, for it is natural that the old should extol the days of their youth; the

weak, the time of their strength; the sick, the season of their vigor; and the disappointed, the spring-tide of their hopes."

That is an elegant way to express some harsh truth. Over the course of 40 or 50 years, time transports us into a future that doesn't look much like the past. Can you imagine how the world looked in 1895 versus 1945? Not only does the external world change tremendously, we change, too. Then age takes away the glorious attributes of youth. Are the good old days as good as you remember? Maybe or maybe not.

Derek Bok
American author and former president of Harvard in the 1970s and 1980s. Born 1930.

"If you think education is expensive, try ignorance."

Man, are we learning this lesson now in America! Just watch some interviews of random people on the street or at the beach. There are Americans roaming around today who think there are 100 states, the Civil War was between the Nazis and the Germans, or Abraham Lincoln was the first black president. Yes, those are actual answers I have heard given by random people questioned in street interviews. Insufficient knowledge leads to illogical decisions.

Napoleon Bonaparte
Military commander and political leader during the French Revolution. One of the most successful generals in history and self-proclaimed Emperor of France. 1769 to 1821

"The best way to keep one's word is to not give it."

I'm not recommending to never promise anything to anyone. However, I would say that we need to be careful about what we promise. Breaking your promises to friends, family, or business associates will lead to partial or complete distrust in you – something that is not going to win you any friends or strengthen any family ties. On the flip side, if you are sure you can deliver on a promise and it is important to make that promise, then go for it. Make the promise, and deliver on it, if at all possible.

"Glory is fleeting, but obscurity is forever."

I think his point is: You might as well go for the glory, even if it is short-lived, because the alternative is permanent obscurity. He wanted some time in the sun, even if was to be a short time. If you desire fame or glory, go for it. What do you have to lose?

"Four hostile newspapers are more to be feared than a thousand bayonets."

It's interesting that the media was effectively molding the minds of the masses over 200 years ago. Even the greatest general of his day was afraid of what it might say.

"There are only two forces in the world, the sword and spirit. In the long-run the sword will always be conquered by the spirit."

Napoleon knew that war is always a temporary condition. Eventually the attitudes and mindsets of the people involved will win out. If the people will tolerate a dictator, they will probably be ruled by one. If their spirit will not tolerate a dictator, then the people will overthrow any dictatorships.

"Religion is what keeps the poor from murdering the rich."

I doubt that is the only thing, but I think there is something to his statement. This is a really interesting notion to consider. What *does* keep people from raping, pillaging, plundering, and murdering unrestrained? Is it their own innate moral compass, lessons learned from their parents, the expectations of their community, fear of government punishment, or fear of eternal damnation? The answer probably varies from person to person and is a different combination of those factors in each case.

Dietrich Bonhoeffer
German Lutheran Pastor and anti-Nazi dissident who was
hanged by the National Socialist (Na-zi) regime near the end of
World War II. 1906 to 1945

**"Silence in the face of evil is itself evil. God will not hold us
guiltless. Not to speak is to speak. Not to act is to act."**

This is similar to the well-known, yet anonymous quote,
"The only thing necessary for evil to triumph in the world
is that good men do nothing." Of course, doing nothing is
normally the easiest thing to do, and hence, it happens a lot.
Furthermore, saying anything against modern group-think
is a fast path to public shaming and maybe losing
everything you have. Evil tends to run wild these days in
the face of the silent and inactive.

Christian Nestell Bovee
New York based writer, a friend and contemporary of several of
the best known writers of the 1800s. 1820 to 1904

**"We unconsciously imitate what pleases us and
approximate to the characters we most admire."**

You have probably heard the old saying, "Monkey see,
monkey do." I think the younger you are, the more true
this is. This idea of consciously (and even unconsciously)
becoming the characters we most admire is the reason why
it is so important to choose your role models carefully,
especially for young people still developing their
personalities.

Russell Brand
A 21st century British comedian, actor, and popular podcaster.
Born 1975.

**"People who say that no change is necessary are the people
who benefit from things staying the same."**

Good point. There is so much propaganda today. It's
unfortunate that we can't just watch and read and learn.

Now we have to first consider who is producing this broadcast, podcast, or article, and what is their motivation. Are they telling me something true and useful, or are they telling me something false and manipulative? Are they pushing a narrative or selling me a product?

"Be led by your talent, not by your self-loathing; those other things you just have to manage."

This is an idea you will find repeated amongst great teachers – the idea of finding your talent and focusing on it. What if Tiger Woods never took up golf or Thomas Edison never invented anything? What if Tom Hanks ran a fast food restaurant instead of making movies? Find your talent, grow it, promote it, and follow it where it leads.

"There is apparently in our modern world, with its surfeit [excess] of information, no objective truth, simply a series of narratives that can be utilized to facilitate power."

Who would have thought 30 or 40 years ago that we would one day be living in a world where the truth is subject to debate and interpretation? There used to be certain sources of information that pretty much everyone trusted. (Maybe they shouldn't have.) Years ago, we perceived that there were objective undeniable facts about the universe, the economy, biology, the populace, and a million other things. However, due to the internet and our computers' ability to generate infinite new and conflicting data, we are sort of living in a modern Tower of Babel. Perhaps we should call it a "network of babble," where we immediately have to couple the "fact" presented to us with the direction from which the "fact" is coming.

"When the state starts acting like a god, ... cultural edicts and moral truths that it won't allow to be debated or challenged, it has become a de facto god."

When I wrote this, thousands of people were locked up in England (of all places) for what they posted online, behavior you don't normally see from a free society. I don't think the US Constitution envisions or allows for a god like that, as it specifically states, "Congress shall make no law respecting an establishment of religion, or prohibiting the free exercise thereof; or abridging the freedom of speech..." However, during the arc of my life, I have seen a huge clamp down on individual rights, first on the freedom of religion, and then on the freedom of speech. Hopefully, we can maintain the freedom of our thoughts. I suggest that everyone read the book *1984*. If it has been more than ten years since you read it, consider reading it again.

William F. Buckley
Founder of *The National Review* and well-known political commentator in his day. 1925 to 2008

"Life is the art of drawing without an eraser."

I like this analogy. In life most things cannot be undone. You cannot un-crash your car or un-say the words you've said. There is no eraser for most of the mistakes we'll make. Hence, we have to slow down, think ahead, and be a little more careful. My wife would tell you that this advice applies to me more than 99% of the population. It's true. Time and time again, at least for me, acting too quickly becomes acting too dangerously. I will never forget the advice my favorite University of Illinois professor gave on the last day of his real estate class: "You will make mistakes; just don't make ones big enough to end your investing career." Therefore, take some risks, but remember that you don't have an eraser.

"Idealism is fine, but as it approaches reality, the costs become prohibitive."

People speak of the idealism of youth. Historically, the young were the ones who tended to question why we can't all live in a utopia, with total peace, harmony, fairness, and equality, devoid of evil. Well, most of them grow up and find out why – the humans who run the place are not perfect. If you pursue a path of printing an infinite number of dollars to solve an infinite number of problems, inflation causes the cost of necessary products to become more than the population can bear.

"There is an inverse relationship between reliance on the state and self-reliance."

This is one of those statements that is self-evident. When you think about it, it must be true. The more you are relying on the government for solutions, the less you are trying to solve your own problems. The other day I heard a pithy thought about self-defense: "When seconds count, the police are only minutes away." True. The police are great, and we are lucky there are people willing to do that job, but you just might have to defend yourself during the three minutes it takes for them to drive to your house.

Buddha
Siddhartha Gautama is commonly referred to as the Buddha. He was a wandering religious teacher and philosopher, who lived in South Asia during the 6th and 5th century BC and founded Buddhism, a religion with about 500 million followers today.

"Thousands of candles can be lit from a single candle, and the life of the candle will not be shortened. Happiness never decreases by being shared."

Think about how inexpensive and easy it would be for you to tell someone today that you appreciate them and that they always do a great job. You could tell them the positive, admirable qualities you have witnessed within them. How easy would it be to light a little candle of happiness for someone today?

"Vigilant among the negligent, wide awake among the sleeping, the wise one advances, like a swift horse leaving a weak one behind."

Fair or not fair, those who are vigilant, thoughtful, and seek wisdom are going to outpace their peers. The Buddha made an excellent argument for why you should read this book, and he did it 2,500 years ago.

"Like someone pointing to treasure is the wise person who sees your faults and points them out."

No one wants to tell their friends and loved ones about their errors or faults. It's human nature. Why risk hurting the feelings of someone you love? But, if you think about it, the best favor you can do for them is to honestly and sincerely point out errors that are correctable and faults that can be worked on. Help them shore up weaknesses and get stronger and better. On the flipside, try to appreciate the friends who went out on a limb and told you something you did not want to hear.

"As a solid mass of rock is not moved by the wind, so a sage is unmoved by praise or blame."

This is tough. Be thankful and grateful for praise. Be contrite and ask for forgiveness when you are indeed guilty. However, when you have a mission and you know you are on the right path, never let the want of praise or the fear of blame take you off course.

"Don't speak harshly to anyone; what you say will be said back to you."

You have heard of karma, right? I do believe when you treat people poorly, your odds of receiving poor treatment in return go way up, not just from that person but also from the people they know and beyond. A negative feedback loop grows and spreads. Help yourself out, along with society at large. To the best of your abilities break the cycle of pain. Be kind and civilized to people, even people who don't deserve it.

"You should follow a good, intelligent person who is wise, insightful, learned, committed to virtue, dutiful, and noble, as the moon follows the path of the stars."

Be very careful whom you choose for a mentor, and hold that teacher to a higher standard than others. Once you can verify the good character of a mentor or teacher, then open your mind to follow their lessons and examples.

"Conquer anger with non-anger; conquer wickedness with goodness; conquer stinginess with giving and a liar with truth."

It's easy to stoop down to the levels of the wicked who attack you, and then fight on their level, but it's so much better to win those battles with peace, goodness, charity, and truth. It's the light that endures and teaches the right lessons to all parties involved.

"If you find an intelligent companion, a fellow traveler, a sage of good conduct, you should travel together, delighted and mindful, overcoming all dangers."

I really like this travel metaphor. I imagine two friends who respect and trust each other moving through life together, helping each other overcome all problems and challenges. This is a goal I have for myself and my friends – a never ending mutual vigilance and beneficial partnership.

"Oneself, indeed, is one's own protector. One does, indeed, make one's own destiny. Therefore, control yourself as a merchant controls a fine horse."

You could view yourself as both a product and a keeper of that product. You have one or more sets of skills, and you need to stay mentally and physically healthy to achieve whatever purpose your life calls for. Find your destiny, pursue it, and also protect yourself along the way.

<u>Charles Bukowski</u>
German-American poet who shared the hard truths of life.
1920 to 1994

I was walking through a bookstore many years ago, and the title of one of his books stopped me in my tracks. I knew I needed to read it because the title elegantly stated something important we should all remember as often as possible. The title was…

"The Days Run Away Like Wild Horses Over the Hills."

How many times do you lie down in bed and think to yourself, *Wasn't I just doing this a couple of hours ago?* Another day has flown by. The older you get, the faster time seems to go, as out of control as wild horses in a dust cloud. I think this happens because every day and every week becomes a smaller and smaller percentage of your life. The challenge is to somehow find a way to slow it all down, live in the moment, enjoy the now, and do important things with your precious limited time.

"We're all going to die, all of us, what a circus! That alone should make us love each other, but it doesn't. We are terrorized and flattened by trivialities; we are eaten up by nothing."

This doesn't need an explanation – just a harsh truth to keep in mind. It's hard to do, but we must constantly remind ourselves to keep the trivialities trivial.

<u>James Mark Burnett</u>
British television producer and former president of MGM Worldwide Television Group. Born 1960.

"There's nothing like biting off more than you can chew, and then chewing anyway."

It doesn't always work, but sometimes when we take on more than we think we are capable of, we discover that our limits are beyond our understanding. The last fairly high peak I climbed was Tenmile Peak outside of Frisco Colorado, probably in 2012. I went with a novice hiker, and as we climbed I kept thinking, *There is no way we are getting up to that peak today.* Yet, we agreed to just keep climbing higher until we couldn't climb anymore. Eventually, we found ourselves at the peak looking down on Frisco. The challenge of getting back down safely was still yet to be conquered, but we made it. I'm sure you have your own stories of doing more than you thought you were capable of. Why not aim uncomfortably high? Most of the time a failure is not life or death; it's just a temporary setback before your next success.

John Burroughs
American naturalist author and important player in the conservation movement. 1837 to 1921

"For anything worth having one must pay the price, and the price is always work, patience, love, and self-sacrifice – no paper currency, no promises to pay, but the gold of real service."

It is certainly true that we appreciate something much more when we work for it than when we receive it for free. Burroughs reminds us that there is a price to pay to achieve something exceptional, and he even spells out that price. It seems to me that our tolerance for sacrifice has waned quite a bit in the last 100 years.

Robert Burton
Oxford University author and scholar, primarily in the field of mathematics. 1577 to 1640

"Don't be penny wise and pound foolish."

This warning is aimed at people who get bogged down worrying about tiny expenditures, while being careless and wasteful with bigger amounts. You won't find too many people like that. Normally, people are consistently wasteful with all amounts of money or conscientious with every expenditure. Where I find this phrase a more useful reminder, at least in business, is failing to invest in better tools, better machines, and better people. For instance, you can leave an old computer in place for 10 years without upgrades in order to save money, but it's probably running at two-thirds the speed of a new one and wasting a tremendous amount of employee hours and effort. You're losing $50,000/year in productivity to postpone a $1,500 expenditure. That's penny wise and pound (or dollar) foolish.

Samuel Butler
A 19th century English novelist. 1835 to 1902

"God cannot alter the past, but historians can."

A good reminder of the power we inadvertently hand over to historians and other keepers of history – the power to change our perception of reality by omitting history, modifying history, fabricating new "history," or suggesting that people tear down statues. It's a crime against humanity to bury realities that we all need to learn from, so that we may avoid the mistakes of the past.

Robert Byrne
American author and champion pool player. 1930 to 2016

"A memorial service is a farewell party for someone who has already left."

That is an interesting point. Have you ever pondered the purpose of a funeral? Is it a final chance to honor someone's life, a collective closure event, a chance to commiserate the loss of a loved one, a final goodbye, or something else? After going to many of these, including both of my parents' funerals, I think the end of life should be handled well. If you would like to honor someone's incredible impactful life, please do that while they are alive. There is a reason that they bring the live actors and musicians to the Kennedy Center to honor them, rather than having a Kennedy Center funeral. Maybe write something like a eulogy for your loved ones while they are still alive, and share it with them. It will probably be one of sweetest things they have ever read. Beyond that, I think someone should speak at the funeral who knew the deceased very well, not just a random pastor or priest. The other funeral attendees need the real life story, not a generic one. Lastly, use this opportunity for forgiveness, not just for the deceased, but for anyone there who has wronged you. What better event than a funeral to remind you of the brevity of life. Don't waste it harboring anger.

Callimachus
Callimachus was an ancient Greek poet, scholar, and librarian who was active in Alexandria during the 3rd century BC.
ca. 310 BC to 240 BC

"A big book is a big bore."

I know some people don't mind reading *War and Peace*, but for the rest of us with shorter attention spans, I have limited this book to an average size. Hopefully, it is digestible by readers with an average tolerance for pain, or maybe we should call it an average tolerance for "work."

James Cameron
Canadian filmmaker with many blockbuster films to his credit. Second highest grossing filmmaker in history at this time. Born 1954.

"If you set your goals ridiculously high and it's a failure, you will fail above everyone else's success."

I like this idea of aiming high, even higher than what one should reasonably aim. The only problem I see with it is finding contentment and gratitude with falling short. If you decide you would like to have $10 million by 50 years old, and you end up with only $5 million, you should not mope about and languish in abject failure. It can be tricky to continue striving for more while also maintaining contentment and gratitude for what you already have.

<u>George Carlin</u>
American comedian, actor, author, and long-time observer of
society. 1937 to 2008

**"A house is just a place to keep your stuff, while you go out
and get more stuff."**

> I am guilty of the crime of too much stuff. The back
> story... It's hard when you are raised by children of the
> Great Depression, especially when you grow up in a trailer
> park. On the one hand, your parents won't throw anything
> away if it just might be useful. On the other hand, you and
> your friends in the trailer park don't have much, but what
> little you have is always subject to being stolen by your
> neighbors. As a result, I am hard-wired to save anything
> useful, acquire more of it if possible, maintain it forever,
> and protect it at all cost. One trait that I hope is getting
> better in America is the obsession with acquiring too many
> things – one reason for the improvement is the minimalist
> mindset of millennials, and the other is the increasing cost
> of things. I think most Americans, including myself, would
> be happier with more time, richer experiences, and fewer
> things.

**"Never argue with an idiot. They will only bring you down
to their level and beat you with experience."**

> Yes, this is a lesson that we all learn one way or another.
> Idiots have a lot of experience arguing with other idiots.
> Superior logic does not matter to them. Think about trying
> to reason with a bully. You're wasting your time with logic
> and reason; a bully only understands force. If you want to
> get through to him, you'll probably have to use force,
> unfortunately. Furthermore, arguing with someone who is
> both ignorant and closed-minded is a complete waste of
> your time. If you're going to get anywhere, you'll have to
> open their closed mind first and then work on their
> ignorance.

"Some people see things that are and ask, 'Why?' Some people dream of things that never were and ask, 'Why not?' Some people have to go to work and don't have time for all that."

A lot of the inventors and artists of yesteryear only had the time to pursue science and art because they were personally born to wealth, or because a wealthy patron supported them. How many more important inventors and artists would there have been across time, if they did not have to dig canals and work in mines, bogged down by the want of sustenance. If you are now one of the fortunate, who has control over your time and effort, please step back and ask yourself, "Am I pursuing the goals that are actually important to me and my family or even perhaps useful to the world?" I believe it is important to be productive in order to feed ourselves and our families, but we also need to find a time and a place to feed our souls, to practice creativity, and to follow our dreams.

Thomas Carlyle
Nineteenth century Scottish essayist, historian, and philosopher. 1795 to 1881

"Instead of saying that man is the creature of circumstance, it would be nearer the mark to say that man is the architect of circumstance. It is character that builds an existence out of circumstance. From the same materials one man builds palaces; one warehouses, another villas. Bricks and mortar are mortar and bricks until the architect can make them something else."

There are countless stories of orphans who became millionaires. There is even a handful of billionaires who grew up in poverty, such as Larry Ellison, Jack Ma, or Oprah Winfrey. I know for a fact that people can overcome meager circumstances, and I love to see them do it. We can start with one circumstance and change it into another. We can be the architects of our own lives if we put in the thought, sweat, and hours.

"The block of granite, which is an obstacle in the pathway of the weak, becomes a stepping-stone in the pathway of the strong."

This quote makes me think of some boulder fields that I crossed in Colorado when I was younger. If you are not walking well, you are not getting through the boulder field, but if you are agile, you'll hop right through it without a problem. It also makes me think of an approach that I applied to obstacles when my staff presented difficult problems to me. When you come to an obstacle, there are four ways to pass it: over it, under it, around it, or through it. My mindset was always, "We will overcome the obstacle; we are just in the process of figuring out how." One way or another, turn those obstacles into stepping-stones.

Andrew Carnegie
Scottish-born American industrialist and philanthropist. He grew up in a one-room cottage, and in 1901 he owned the first $1 billion corporation in the world, U.S. Steel. 1835 to 1919

"There is no use whatever trying to help people who do not help themselves. You cannot push anyone up a ladder, unless he be willing to climb himself."

We want to be able to push some folks up a ladder, especially loved ones and relatives. It just doesn't work. A psychology professor (and foundation director) told me that he believed motivation was 80% intrinsic. You can do a few things to try and motivate people, but most of it comes from within. Hence, when someone sincerely asks for your help and is willing to make an effort, you can probably help them. Otherwise, you are wasting your time.

Dale Carnegie
Author of *How to Win Friends and Influence People* and several other books on self-improvement. 1888 to 1955

"Success is getting what you want. Happiness is wanting what you have."

This is one of my all-time favorite quotes. I first came across it during college and then kept it on my wall until I graduated. The first part is easy to understand, but the second half is a bit perplexing. What does it mean to want what you have? I think it's just another way to say that you are grateful for what you have. You are not coveting what others have but rather reveling in your own situation and enjoying your own possessions to the fullest. Many of us move through life desiring all kinds of things and possibly obtaining them. We often find that they don't bring the happiness we expected. Buddhists believe that desire is the source of all suffering. This is why the Buddhist monks try not to crave material goods. I'm not suggesting we live like monks, but I will firmly testify that having too many possessions can cause suffering. It's too much to clean, organize, repair, store, protect, and worry about. We can remove some of our suffering, and even find satisfaction, by desiring what we already have. For most of us, what we already have is enough. Gratitude for the abundance in your life is a better mindset than to harbor discontent for some kind of scarcity.

"When fate hands you a lemon, make lemonade."

I said this not long ago to a farmer. A city bulldozed two acres of trees on one of my properties without asking for permission. They had no good reason, and it wasn't even legal. I considered whether there was a way to turn this lemon into lemonade. After pondering it for a while, I asked the farmer to plant soybeans on the newly cleared acres, which he did. Then I increased the tillable acres in his lease by two acres. Lemonade.

"You can make more friends in two months by becoming interested in other people than you can in two years by trying to get other people interested in you."

This is one of those weird inversions in the world. If you are interested in having someone for a friend, human nature motivates you to sell yourself to this potential friend, but that doesn't work. In fact, it's more likely that you will run

the fellow or lady off. A better approach is to become
sincerely interested in the potential friend. They will
hopefully feel the sincerity and appreciate having someone
to listen to them and care about their problems.

Lewis Carroll
Actually named Charles Lutwidge Dodgson, he was an English
mathematician, photographer, and author of several works such
as Alice's Adventures in Wonderland. 1832 to 1898

**"If you don't know where you are going, any road will get
you there."**

By logic, this must be true. Therefore, you need to develop
a destination in your mind before you set out on a journey.
You need at least some route in mind, along with a precise
destination. Unfortunately, I meet a lot of people who
seem to have no destination in mind. They're just drifting
into an unknown future.

George Washington Carver
American agricultural scientist, inventor, and professor at the
Tuskegee Institute. 1864 to 1943

**"I love to think of nature as an unlimited broadcasting
station, through which God speaks to us every hour, if we
will only tune in."**

There is something magical or spiritual in the high
mountains, deep valleys, wide rivers, and vast oceans. We
need to regularly commune with nature and remind
ourselves where we come from. One good way to stay
grounded is by literally touching the ground.

"Where there is no vision, there is no hope."

When we fail to look forward and visualize the future that
we want for ourselves, we cease moving towards that
future.

Wilt Chamberlain
American basketball player, who was 7'1", and is still the only
pro player to score 100 points in a single game. 1936 to 1999

"Nobody roots for Goliath."

>   I included this quote because in America we tend to root
>   for the underdog. From the fan perspective, it's fine to
>   watch the biggest players dominate the smaller ones, but
>   it's captivating to see the smallest guy in a competition find
>   a way to win. Additionally, when we are actually in a
>   competition, we tend to resent the players who are bigger
>   and better than we are. Sometimes you may find yourself
>   in the position of Goliath in your work life, in the gym, at
>   school, within your extended family, or in some other
>   venue. In those times remember that, by nature, not
>   everyone is wishing you well.

Edwin Hubbel Chapin
American preacher, speaker, and poet. 1814 to 1880

"Out of suffering have emerged the strongest souls."

>   I suppose a few lucky people led a charmed life from
>   beginning to end, but the vast majority of them came
>   through some period of struggle, just like you and me.
>   They were baptized or forged by fire. I think a degree of
>   adversity is good for setting priorities, clarifying reality,
>   promoting gratitude, and generally teaching one how to
>   fight through difficult times.

Geoffrey Chaucer
14th century poet, philosopher, author of the famous
Canterbury Tales, and member of parliament. ca. 1343 to 1400

"Time and tide wait for no man."

>   I don't know about you, but many times in my life I have
>   wished for the supernatural power to stop time. To snap
>   my fingers and pause everything would be so incredible.

Sometimes I just throw up my hands and exclaim, *Enough; I can't keep up with everyone and everything that is demanding my time.* However, time doesn't care if you can keep up with your obligations or not. It keeps rolling forward like the current of a river. So, how can you better keep up with your obligations? Work faster, work harder, or better yet, work smarter. You can also off-load some obligations. Pare down your life until you feel like you have it under control.

"Love is blind."

When you truly love someone, that love may overcome how they look, how they act, their pedigree, education, wealth, or any other personal characteristic that may make them disagreeable to the next person.

Lord Chesterfield (Philip Dormer Stanhope)
18th century British diplomat and politician. 1694 to 1773

"A weak mind is like a microscope, which magnifies trifling things but cannot receive great ones."

One challenge we all face is how to strike a balance between how much attention to give to details and how much to give to the big picture. We all have a natural-born propensity to focus more on one or the other. Chesterfield seems to believe that it's only the weak-minded who magnify trifling things, but I have certainly met some intelligent people who do the same. Maybe we should say that it's a weak approach to magnify trivialities and ignore larger concepts. I have found that for any difficult project, I need to first visualize the larger end result, and then tend to dozens or hundreds of details to reach that end result. There can be 24,000 dots that comprise a picture, but without the little dots there is no picture.

Winston Churchill
Well-known, well-loved British statesman who was a member of Parliament for over 60 years and Prime Minister during World War II and again in the 1950's. 1874 to 1965

"History will be kind to me for I intend to write it."

That is an excellent strategy. If you want history to remember you well, write the history yourself or write a good autobiography to leave for posterity.

"When you are going through hell, keep going."

This is one of those quotes you should memorize and keep handy at all times. I like to remember it as, "When you are walking through hell, keep walking." Either way, it's a clever reminder not to sit down and give up when times are tough. When we are suffering physically or mentally from the challenges that life throws at us, there are better days ahead if we persist. Keep in mind that life inevitably gets better after it gets worse. That's how cycles work, at least until you face your final battle, which will not be today.

"Responsibility is the price of greatness."

This is not a small price, and it is not a price that most people want to pay. Can you imagine having hundreds, thousands, or millions of lives depending on the decisions that you are making? Unless you are a sociopath (someone who cares nothing for others), it must be a heavy responsibility.

"It has been said that democracy is the worst form of government, except all the others that have been tried."

My opinion is that monarchies work well for monarchs, and communist dictatorships work well for communist dictators and their close friends. The best chance a commoner has to live well is in a capitalistic democracy. You still have the risk that some low-information, illogical voters will make bad decisions or vote themselves a limitless supply of fiat currency. However, at least in a democracy there is a chance to realize mistakes and correct them. There is a chance to remove despots without a bloody revolution.

<u>Cicero</u>
Marcus Tullius Cicero was a Roman philosopher who was
widely read and admired by the founding fathers of America.
106 BC to 43 BC

**"Gratitude is not only the greatest of virtues, but the parent
of all the others."**

It's so easy to lose gratitude when faced with day-to-day
troubles, yet gratitude is a fundamental base for happiness.
Think about all of the horrible physical ailments that you or
your family could be facing. Think about living in the
middle of a war or a natural disaster. Imagine going
hungry for years or spending decades in prison. The odds
of you even being born were about <u>1 in 400 trillion</u>. So,
try, try, try to focus on the blessings and remember them
every day. You are so lucky and blessed!

"More is lost by indecision than wrong decision."

I have also heard it stated in this form: "Indecision is more
dangerous than decision". I love this quote and remind
myself and others of it repeatedly. I envision someone
walking halfway into a busy street and then questioning
whether or not to go all the way across or turn back. That's
the person who is going to be hit by a car. Indecision can
literally become fatal, so make the best decision you can,
and then execute it quickly and thoroughly.

"The life of the dead is placed in the memory of the living."

I think Cicero is saying that our ancestors and friends can
live on through us. They affect our character, our morals,
our knowledge, our skills, and many other things. We are
all products of our DNA and our experiences to date, and
those we knew and miss are still here with us in a variety of
ways.

**"Any man can make mistakes, but only an idiot persists in
his error."**

Have you ever persisted in an error? I certainly have. Our challenge is to step back occasionally, notice it happening, and then change course. We need to stay open to the constructive criticism that can come from a friend or even a stranger. We need to listen for that voice that says, "Pssst. You're being an idiot, repeatedly."

"Cultivation to the mind is as necessary as food to the body."

Learning and growing your mind should be a lifetime work, not just something you did in school, maybe long ago. The brain needs to be exercised to remain strong and healthy.

"It is the peculiar quality of a fool to perceive the faults of others and to forget his own."

When you observe a fool in action, realize that he often doesn't understand or see his foolishness, and maybe he never will. You can choose to try to correct the fool or choose not to waste your time.

"The function of wisdom is to discriminate between good and evil."

I would argue that wisdom has many more functions, but this is certainly an important one. We live in kind of an absurd time when some people think it's evil to call something evil. For thousands of years, we understood and pretty much agreed on what constituted evil, but the internet Tower of Babel has confused us on the matter. Every action is OK with a certain online community and should be tolerated. If you think it isn't, you are being too judgemental and need to have your thoughts corrected.

Confucius

Confucius was a Chinese philosopher who lived from 551 BC until about 479 BC. His teachings and philosophies are fundamental to east Asian culture. Confucianism is concerned with inner virtue, morality, and respect for the community. *The Analects of Confucius* is an anthology of his teachings, and there is quite a bit of wisdom within it. Here are selected pieces of wisdom from the Analects.

"When you meet someone better than yourself, turn your thoughts to becoming his equal."

Jealousy is the basis for so much evil: theft, lies, violence, etc. Never harbor jealousy in your heart. It doesn't do anything to diminish the object of your jealously, and at a minimum, it wastes your time and energy. Re-route that jealous energy into motivation to improve yourself and your own situation. Focus on who you are and what you need to do to be more like the people who are better than yourself.

"When you make a mistake, do not be afraid of mending your ways."

This seems simple and easy, but so many folks are afraid of admitting their mistakes or being seen as wrong. They imagine that they need to maintain some kind of aura of perfection. That's impossible, and everyone with significant life experience knows it. I have found that admitting mistakes, and committing to correcting those mistakes quickly, is the fastest and best path to overcome the damage from errors.

"I am a fortunate man. Whenever I make a mistake, other people are sure to notice it."

This is obviously a joke, but there is wisdom in it. When people point out your mistakes, you could be shocked, embarrassed, and feel ashamed, or you could frame it differently in your mind… "Thank you so much for noticing this mistake sooner rather than later. I'll correct it immediately, minimize the damage, and try not repeat it." That's useful. That makes you stronger.

"The common people can be made to follow a path but not to understand it."

Here we are again. It sounds like Confucius is talking about today, but he said it 2,500 years ago. With the out-of-control marriage of big-tech and mass media, many people are following a lot of paths that they do not understand. How can we fix this? That's a difficult question, but I would at least advise not to walk down any path until you've studied it from every angle and tried your very best to understand it. Any path suggested for you should stand up to your own logic and world experience.

"Do not accept as friends anyone who is not as good as you."

I don't believe this is as literal as it seems. He means "good" in terms of behaviors like honesty and integrity, rather than traits like physical strength or musical ability. I agree that we do need to be very careful about choosing friends because they affect our lives in profound and fundamental ways.

"Make it your guiding principle to do your best for others and to be trustworthy in what you say."

These two ideas were fundamental to my business growing every year for over 20 years. Customers notice when you are doing your best for them and when you prove yourself worthy of their trust.

"Do not impose on others what you yourself do not desire."

It's the golden rule stated in the negative, about 500 years before Jesus.

"He who wishes to secure the good of others has already secured his own."

I think Confucius is saying that if your mind is focused on the right things, such as taking care of others before yourself, then your soul is on the correct spiritual path.

"Our greatest glory is not in never falling, but in rising every time we fall."

You can find countless individuals in history who had a few failures before their great success. You are not a failure, unless you let some failure stop you from trying for the rest of your life. If you get back up off the floor and re-engage, you're a fighter, not a failure.

"To know what is right and not do it is the worst cowardice."

I think it would be difficult to stand by and watch injustice without raising your voice or raising your hand to it, yet some people do it and film it with their cell phone. When you see something you know is not right and do nothing to help someone suffering, that's probably something you'll never forget. It diminishes you.

"Acquire new knowledge whilst thinking over the old, and you may become a teacher of others."

Acquiring new knowledge is fundamental to our growth, but we also need to revisit and remember what we have already learned. Let your knowledge compound, not just for your own benefit, but for the benefit of others. You may not have ever thought of yourself as a teacher, but in a way, we are all teaching someone, whether it's our kids, siblings, parents, friends, or coworkers.

"Study the past if you would divine the future."

We never know for sure what the future holds, but the best chance we have at guessing what is to come is to understand history. We can recognize how current conditions compare to historical conditions and remember what happened the last time. According to Mark Twain, "History does not repeat itself, but it often rhymes."

"He who gives no thought to difficulties in the future is sure to be beset by worries much closer at hand."

When I managed some low-income housing for a year in the late 1990s, I saw first-hand what happens to people who give no thought to the future. They quickly become homeless. I am not advocating that you spend all of your time worrying about the future, but there is a requisite amount of future planning and preparation to keep your life improving rather than deteriorating.

"The gentleman [leader] is generous without it costing him anything, works others hard without their complaining, has desires without being greedy, is casual without being arrogant, and is awe-inspiring without appearing fierce."

Confucius is laying out traits here of the sort of leader that people want to follow, a leader who gets the mission done. When I was in an organizational behavior class, the professor said that a good manager demonstrates both discipline (for the benefit of the people above him) and consideration to the people below him. It seems like Confucius figured out the importance of balance in leadership long ago.

Stephen Covey
Educator, speaker, and author of *Seven Habits of Highly Effective People*, as well as many other works between 1970 and 2012. 1932 to 2012

"Seek first to understand, then to be understood."

By my estimation, the majority of communication does not happen this way in the world. Most of it starts with: "you need to understand, I don't know why you can't understand, you are crazy if you believe," or another non-empathetic stance. We will get farther with our communication by starting with a genuine request to understand the other side's position. Start with something like, "I would like to hear what you think about X." Even if the other side's position is diametrically opposed to your own, they will certainly appreciate being heard and probably be more open to hear your ideas in response.

"If we keep doing what we're doing, we're going to keep getting what we're getting."

I think this is almost always true. Covey means that if you are failing to achieve a goal, taking the same action over and over again will result in failure over and over again. It's common sense, but it's something we should be reminded of periodically. Creative problem solving means changing your approach and continuing to change it until you find the right solution.

"Begin with the end in mind."

Beginning without the end in mind is like starting a trip by leaving your house in a random direction. You are going to waste a lot of time and probably never get to anywhere you want to be.

William Cowper
English poet and hymn writer who lived 1731 to 1800.

"Variety's the spice of life, that gives it all its flavor."

I love to try new things and visit new places, and I always have. How can you properly assess what your favorite things are without understanding all the options? Keep your life fresh and spicy with the never-ending variety this huge world has to offer.

Marie Curie
Nobel prize winning Polish physicist who discovered Radium and Polonium. She paved the way for the use of radiation in medicine, including treatments for cancer. 1867 to 1934

"Be less curious about people and more curious about ideas."

Eleanor Roosevelt said something similar to this that I have never forgotten since I heard it many years ago. "Great minds discuss ideas; average minds discuss events; small minds discuss people." (See page 191.) The next time you partake in gossiping about an individual, consider whether you are pursuing greatness or just being small-minded. Discussing ideas takes more effort and requires taking the risk that your ignorance might be exposed. Heck, you might even have to change your mind about a topic if someone else points out the errors in your logic.

"You cannot build a better world without improving the individuals."

I learned over the years that a company is only a collection of individual employees, and even one bad individual can bring down the entire organization's productivity and morale. Likewise, we'll need to improve a lot of the eight billion individuals living in the world today if we hope to have a better world. Does it seem to you that the average person you meet has been getting smarter, stronger, and healthier over time?

Dalai Lama
Tenzin Gyatzo, the 14th Dalai Lama, is a spiritual leader of the Tibetan people. Born 1935.

"Our prime purpose in this life is to help others. And if you can't help them, at least don't hurt them."

This seems like a noble aspiration. Odds are, you have been hurt by others, either purposefully or accidentally. Don't be part of the problem; be part of the solution. Help others if you can, and try not to hurt anyone.

"Where ignorance is our master, there is no possibility of real peace."

Hence, we see a lot of places in the world without peace. Ignorance abounds. How to replace the noise and ignorance with clarity and logic will be a challenge for humanity in the decades and maybe centuries ahead.

"We can never obtain peace in the outer world until we make peace with ourselves."

I think you will find this idea frequently repeated by the wisest teachers. It's kind of like putting on your own oxygen mask, in the event of an airplane emergency, before putting your child's mask on. You have to have peace within you before you can share it with others.

"Old friends pass away, new friends appear. It is just like the days. An old day passes, a new day arrives. The important thing is to make it meaningful: a meaningful friend or a meaningful day."

Now that I have lost several friends and lived many days, more and more I appreciate the value of each friend and each day. Old friends and old days can't be bought, and they can't be replaced – cherish them and make the most of every day and every friendship.

"Know the rules well, so you can break them effectively."

What a rebel, that Dalai Lama. I agree with his premise. If you have been out there operating in the real world for at least a couple of decades, then you understand this idea. When you really understand a system well, then you know which corners can be cut and which ones cannot. Cut the right corners, and you become hyper-efficient; cut the wrong corners, and you are in jail or bankrupt.

Charles Darwin
Highly influential English naturalist, geologist, and biologist. Author of *On the Origin of Species*. He introduced the idea that evolution resulted from natural selection and survival of the fittest. 1809 to 1882

"A man who dares to waste one hour of time has not discovered the value of life."

I share his sense of urgency. Wasting precious time is a terrible shame, yet we have to be careful how we define the "wasting" of time. Spending time fostering relationships and staying healthy, mentally and physically, is not a waste of time.

"The mystery of the beginning of all things is insoluble by us; and I for one must be content to remain an agnostic."

The mystery of the beginning is still unsolved today. Why is the universe here? Why is there is life within it? We don't know all of the answers and never will, and it's okay to admit that and accept it.

"It is not the strongest of the species that survives, not the most intelligent that survives. It is the one that is the most adaptable to change."

Darwin was an expert on survival, so we should listen to his perspective. We don't necessarily have to be the strongest or smartest but rather the quickest to make positive changes when adversity strikes.

"A man's friendships are one of the best measures of his worth."

I think finding friends, strengthening those relationships, and maintaining them is indeed one of the most important things that we will do in this plane of existence. Virtually everyone who knew my father considered him a friend, and many of them considered him their best friend. After he passed away, so many people approached me and told me that he was their best friend. It made me realize for the first time that you can be a "best friend" to many people at the same time. Darwin saw the limitless value of friendships and made the astute observation that if someone has a lot a great friends, he (or she) is probably a great person.

<u>Leonardo Da Vinci</u>
What more can be said about the world renowned Da Vinci?
He painted the Mona Lisa and the Last Supper and sketched the
Vitruvian Man. He was also a sculptor, inventor, engineer,
cartographer, and biologist who was hundreds of years ahead of
his contemporaries - THE renaissance man. 1452 to 1519

**"As a well-spent day brings happy sleep, so life well-used
brings happy death."**

> Many people spend their lives doing something without
> thinking much about how to spend their lives. I think Da
> Vinci is saying it is good to work hard and use the gifts
> you've been given and the talents you've developed. If you
> do that, you will have no regrets about the way you've
> spent your life.

"Wisdom is the daughter of experience."

> Wisdom can arise from your direct experience or someone
> else's. The point of this book is to bring you wisdom from
> other people's experiences. Learn from the wise sages, so
> that you can make better decisions and maybe avoid some
> suffering.

<u>Miguel De Cervantes</u>
Important 16th and 17th century Spanish novelist, author of
Don Quixote. 1547 to 1616

**"Good actions ennoble us, and we are the sons of our own
deeds."**

> I see this idea recurring frequently amongst the great minds
> in history. The idea is that we are products of the decisions
> and actions we have taken. The college you attend, the
> friends you acquire, and the person you marry all have
> profound effects on the rest of your life. Likewise, when
> faced with a choice between good or evil, the decision you
> make at that juncture may have an enormous effect on the
> rest of your life. Keep this in mind when making important
> decisions.

Rene Descartes
French author, philosopher, mathematician, and scientist. One
of the most important European thinkers of the renaissance.
1596 to 1650

"I think; therefore I am."

You may have heard this in Latin as "Cogito Ergo Sum."
It's one of the most famous quotes in the world. It is
believed that Descartes was trying to give us a way to know
that we exist. If we are sitting here thinking, we must exist.
I have never wondered whether or not I exist, but I have
certainly wondered how the world will know that I existed.

**"The reading of all good books is like a conversation with
the finest minds of past centuries."**

Agreed. To some extent, the thoughts of the finest minds
are available for our examination and study. Why not
spend the time to hear what they have to say?

**"A state is better governed which has few laws, and those
laws strictly observed."**

This is a good point Descartes made around 400 years ago.
If a country keeps making more and more laws without
removing any of them, eventually everything you do is
illegal. Furthermore, the more laws that are made, the
harder it is for anyone to know them all. Case in point: the
Internal Revenue Code and Federal Tax Regulations are
over 10 million words long. Hence, no one knows all of it;
how could they? Besides the logistical difficulty of storing
a vast compendium of laws in your head, there is also the
issue of enforcing that compendium. When the list of laws
becomes too long, enforcement becomes impossible.

**"If you would be a real seeker after truth, it is necessary
that at least once in your life you doubt, as far as possible,
all things."**

Been there, done that, bought the T-shirt. Some believe
that doubt is a sign of weakness, lack of faith, or a kind of
depression that you need to escape. However, I would call
it getting serious or getting real with yourself. It's actually
those who are sure of everything that are delusional.
Today, probably more than ever, things can appear to be
what they are not.

**"It is not enough to have a good mind; the main thing is to
use it well."**

Have you known intelligent people who do little or nothing
with that intelligence? It's kind of tragic, like an incredible
artist who paints no pictures or the woman with the most
beautiful voice in the world who sings no songs. I'm a
believer in finding what you are supposed to do in the
world, and then doing it. Those gifted with great
intelligence should endeavor to accomplish great things for
themselves, their family, and perhaps even humanity.

Peter De Vries
20th century American editor and novelist. 1910 to 1993

**"We are not primarily put on this earth to see through one
another, but to see one another through."**

Helping each other must be one of our purposes. That's
how humans survived millennia ago. They were without
fangs, claws, excessive speed, flight, superior strength,
thick fur, and a host of other animal advantages, but they
had cooperation and love and respect for one another.
They helped each other survive and even thrive.

**"It is the final proof of God's omnipotence that he need not
exist to save us."**

This was clearly something of a joke. I certainly would
never purport to understand the existence or nature of God.
Yet, it is interesting to me to ponder whether irrefutable
definitive proof of God's existence, or lack thereof, would
change the world we live in today.

"Nostalgia isn't what it used to be."

I think he is pointing out that probably nothing is as good as we remember it. We tend to forget our old pain and suffering and cling to the past pleasures and rewards.

"The value of marriage is not that adults produce children but that children produce adults."

You may have seen this in the people you know. A child arrives, and the parent finally gets serious about their career, education, finances, or health. In other words, the new child pushes the old child (their parent) into adulthood.

John Dewey
University philosophy teacher and co-founder of the movement known as Pragmatism.   1859 to 1952

"Education is not preparation for life; education is life itself."

Unfortunately, a number of people see education as something they do through 12th grade or college, and then that's over, and life begins – no more "education" required. However, I feel that every day that we get up and walk through all that life presents to us is an opportunity to learn new things, refine our current understanding, and sharpen our skills. We can learn something new every day of our lives if we try.

"The self is not something ready-made, but something in continuous formation through choice of action."

I like this idea that we are not baked into a permanent mold but rather continuously changing throughout our lives as a result of the decisions we make. Whatever we are now, there is a chance that we can become better through hard work, prudent actions, and maybe a little luck.

Walt Disney
Founder of the Disney empire of cartoons, movies, and theme
parks. 1901 to 1966

"If you can dream it, you can do it."

> Humans have proven this over and over again. They have
> proposed what seemed to be impossible. They have been
> called crazy and irrational, and then they've made the
> impossible possible. So, free your mind to dream, and free
> your hands to build the dream.

"Growing old is mandatory, but growing up is optional."

> The happiest people I have known maintain a youthful
> outlook and youthful sense of awe about the world. They
> play and learn new skills and keep creating. I never worry
> that people may deem me childish or silly or think that I am
> not serious enough. I think we should all strive to feel the
> way we did when we were eight or ten years old and
> anxious to open our Christmas presents.

Benjamin Disraeli
Two-time Prime Minister of the United Kingdom.
1804 to 1881

"The secret of success is constancy to [of] purpose."

> If I had known this secret by 20 years old (instead of 35),
> my twenties would have been much easier. After observing
> many clients and associates for decades, I believe what
> Disraeli said is absolutely true. Most successes you will
> find in life are not the result of a brief foray into an activity;
> they are the result of years of getting up every day focused
> on the mission at hand. Success tends to happen when all
> of your mental and physical strength remains focused on
> achieving the same one goal – no wavering, no distractions,
> and no pause in progress.

Leo Durocher
Professional baseball player, manager, and coach.
1905 to 1991

"I want to achieve immortality by not dying."

> I agree with that same lofty goal, but I haven't yet figured
> out how to get it done. I could be happy living and learning
> new things for at least a thousand years. However, I am a
> bit worried about over-crowding on the planet if everyone
> else does it, too.

Wayne Dyer
American self-help author and well-known motivational
speaker. 1940 to 2015

**"With everything that has happened to you, you can either
feel sorry for yourself or treat what has happened as a gift.
Everything is either an opportunity to grow or an obstacle
to keep you from growing. You get to choose."**

> So many people walk around filled with self-pity. They
> think the bad things that happened in their past have
> permanently limited their happiness and chances for
> success. However, everything that you have experienced
> has led you to right where you are, which may not be as
> bad as you think. Unless you're on your deathbed, there is
> an unknown future out there for you to seize and to live.

Thomas Edison
American inventor who ushered in a great deal of what we
enjoy in the modern world today. He and his team invented
devices for sound recording, motion pictures, electrical power
generation, lighting, and more. He held an incredible 1,093
patents upon his death. 1847 to 1931

**"I have not failed. I've just found 10,000 ways that won't
work."**

What an empowering outlook. Every time you "fail" you do not really fail; you are simply one step closer to success. Use that as motivation to keep trying.

"Our greatest weakness lies in giving up. The most certain way to succeed is always to try just one more time."

Edison is the king of trying until you succeed. If we all had one-tenth of his determination, we would do well.

"We often miss opportunity because it's dressed in overalls and looks like work."

Isn't that the truth today? In America, it seems to me, we are rapidly running out of men and women who are willing and able to get dirty to fix a problem. We are getting short on farmers, plumbers, mechanics, electricians, tree-trimmers, and a host of other skilled laborers. There is great opportunity available for those willing to do the work that others are not willing to do.

"The three great essentials to achieve anything worthwhile are, first, hard work; second, stick-to-itiveness; third, common sense."

These are the essentials that earned one man 1,093 patents. You, too, can use the same concepts to achieve your goals.

"Genius is one percent inspiration, ninety-nine percent perspiration."

This is a fairly well-known quote. Edison has a good point. It's easy to observe someone with tremendous skill and just think that they were lucky to be born with that inherent incredible skill. What you don't see is the perspiration that went into honing that genius's skills over the last 5, 10, or 20 years. Ten thousand hours of practice may have led up to the five minutes that you observed.

"Non-violence leads to the highest ethics, which is the goal of all evolution. Until we stop harming all other living beings, we are still savages."

I don't know if we are ever going to throw off Edison's definition of "savage." I sincerely hope we do evolve towards non-violence. With over 12,000 nuclear warheads still in the world today, the jury is still out.

"There are no rules here – we're trying to accomplish something."

I think Edison was trying to free his staff from preconceived notions and rules. He wanted them to think about and try outside-of-the-box solutions. I'm a big proponent of brain-storming – generating as many ideas as possible without getting bogged down in their perceived viability. Some of the most creative solutions come from this exercise.

"Unfortunately, there seems to be far more opportunity out there than ability.... We should remember that good fortune often happens when opportunity meets with preparation."

This is the norm: there are millions of open jobs available and also millions of unemployed workers. Why? A bunch of people do not possess the skills that are in demand. One of my favorite quotes is "Luck favors the prepared." It's not perfectly accurate. It's not actually luck that favors the prepared but rather opportunity that favors the prepared.

"To do much clear thinking a person must arrange for regular periods of solitude when they can concentrate and indulge the imagination without distraction."

I have heard of other great thinkers calling for this same action, so there must be something to it. How many of us arrange for times of quiet solitude these days? How many of us take time to indulge our imagination? There probably is not enough of this kind of activity.

"Everything comes to him who hustles while he waits."

> If you understand time efficiency, you understand that you
> could always be doing something besides just waiting. You
> could send a productive text, pay a bill, learn something on
> your phone, or call someone you haven't called for a while.
> Don't leave your house to do just one thing. Plan your
> actions, and kill two or three birds with one stone.

Robert C. Edwards

I'm not sure which Robert C. Edwards said this, but it's funny
and poignant regardless.

**"Don't place too much confidence in the man who boasts of
being as honest as the day is long. Wait until you meet him
at night."**

> I wanted to include this because it illustrates something I've
> witnessed during 30 years in business and while working as
> an auditor. As soon as someone says, "You can trust me,"
> that should sound off an alarm bell in your brain. You
> better subject that person to an extra of dose scrutiny. A
> truly trustworthy person does not need to convince you of
> his or her trust-worthiness. They already have a reputation
> that supports their integrity and honesty. It's the shady
> character who goes out of his way to sell you on his
> purported honesty. Even worse is the character who tells
> you, "You can trust me because I'm a Christian." No. I can
> trust you after I observe your consistent integrity. Your
> self-declared Christianity is irrelevant to your actual
> integrity and actual adherence to Christian principles.

Tryon Edwards

American theologian, minister, and author, who lived 1809 to
1894. I really appreciate what this sage had to say in the 19th
century.

**"Thoughts become words, words become deeds, deeds
become habits, habits become character, and character
becomes destiny.**

I think this is a strong lesson about how we build a reputation and character over time, even over a lifetime. That character then greatly influences our destiny in life. Be vigilant about what you are thinking and saying and the habits you develop. They are leading you down a certain path. Is it a good one?

"Between two evils, choose neither; between two goods, choose both."

Absolutely. If possible, when faced with choosing between two evils, choose neither of them. The second part of the quote reminds me of a decision I had to make over 20 years ago. There were two partners in our CPA firm at the time. We were each excited about hiring a new candidate, but we each had a different top candidate in mind. We debated and struggled with the decision until I said, "Let's go for it, and hire them both." That was the right decision, as one of them put in seven good years and the other one is now the managing partner.

"He that never changes his opinions, never corrects his mistakes, and will never be wiser on the morrow than he is today."

I'm not married to an opinion. If I'm wrong, then I'm wrong, and I surely want to know about it. There are a lot of people walking around with their knowledge base solidified and their conclusions all settled. There is no changing their mind. When I meet someone like that, regardless if I agree with them or not, it's an indicator to me that they live in an echo chamber, they've been sheltered from reality, or they're mentally lazy.

"If you would know anything thoroughly, teach it to others."

It is a shame to become an expert on a topic or the master of a skill and then fail to pass along the expertise. We are all standing on so many shoulders now, the inventors of wheels, water filtration, surgery, cars, planes, computers, and a million other concepts. We owe it to our descendants to pass along the knowledge that was passed along to us, plus a little bit more.

"Right actions in the future are the best apologies for bad actions in the past."

I hope this is true. Have you ever wronged someone that you did not intend to? I certainly have. As long as we have some future left, we have a chance to make it up to them.

"People never improve unless they look to some standard or example higher or better than themselves."

When you see someone stronger, faster, smarter, with a nicer house or fancier car, try not to approach that situation with envy. Envy isn't going to do anything other than make you mad. Try to approach it with aspiration. Rather than thinking, *I hate that they have more than I do*, think *That's cool – something for me to aspire towards.* This quote calls us to look to examples better than ourselves. I think this means not just to notice the example, but also to try to match the example, if possible.

Albert Einstein
German theoretical physicist who was widely acknowledged as one of the greatest and most influential physicists of all time. Einstein is best known for developing the theory of relativity. He also made important contributions to the development of the theory of quantum mechanics. Relativity and quantum mechanics are the two pillars of modern physics, and his mass-energy equivalence formula, $E=mc^2$, might be the world's most famous equation. 1879 to 1955

"We can't solve problems by using the same kind of thinking we used when we created them."

This quote is similar to the old saying, "If you find yourself in a hole, stop digging." You should not dwell on mistakes.

You should learn what you can from them and try something different next time.

"If you can't explain it simply, you don't understand it well enough."

This is a lesson for those who give lessons. I have spoken in front of many groups during the last 30 years: business students, small business networking groups, tax and audit training sessions, millionaire classes, and to those interested in my books. I have also attended many more presentations conducted by other presenters. What I have found is this: the best presentations are not detailed on a screen. The audience can easily read bullet points on their own, and if you are going to just stand up there and read off your bullet points, you might as well just email the slides to the audience and skip the whole presentation. The way to give a useful and enjoyable presentation is to know the subject matter inside and out. Put very little on a screen, interact consistently with the audience, and just explain it simply because you know it so well.

"Not everything that can be counted counts, and not everything that counts can be counted.

I think Einstein is saying that we need not track, understand, or worry about every little thing in life. Stay focused on what is important, and that usually can't be calculated with math.

"Insanity is doing the same thing over and over again and expecting different results."

This sounds to me like something a lot of governments do. It's a fairly famous quote and important to remember. When you find yourself trying the same thing over and over again (and failing), realize you are acting crazy and illogical. Try a different approach. Talk to people who have succeeded, and keep varying your approach until you achieve your objective.

"The only source of knowledge is experience."

Maybe he should have specified new knowledge, reliable knowledge, or useful knowledge, rather than just any knowledge. We can certainly look up anything on a search engine these days or read anything in a book, but if you really want to learn something and know the thing well, experience is the way to go. I have spent my life traveling extensively with a goal of soaking up all of the real-life experience that I can get. Good experiences teach you what to do, and bad experiences teach you what not to do.

"Technological progress is like an axe in the hands of a pathological criminal."

What was his point exactly? It's hard to say. However, I have been fearful for many years that man's technology is progressing faster than man's civility. Our ability to store data, manipulate numbers, spread information, and build weapons is running ahead of our ability to judge how and when to use all of those tools.

"Everything should be made as simple as possible, but not simpler."

Achieving simplicity is complex for some or us. Einstein believed in getting things into the simplest possible system, and he was smart enough to do it. You find this idea echoed by many other great thinkers. They have the gift of recognizing undue complexity before getting bogged down in it. Unfortunately, that is a skill I am still working on.

Dwight D. Eisenhower
Supreme commander of the Allied forces in Europe during World War II and 34th President of the United States.
1890 to 1969

"Only our individual faith in freedom can keep us free."

Control of the masses and the suppression of dissent is the norm throughout history and amongst other countries in the world. President Eisenhower recognized and communicated to us that it is only a bunch of individuals in America who hold the key to the freedom of Americans. When enough of us believe in freedom and are willing to protect it, then we have it. Otherwise, we become part of the suppressed masses.

"Though force can protect in emergency, only justice, fairness, consideration, and cooperation can finally lead men to the dawn of eternal peace."

I trust that Eisenhower understood war and peace pretty well (as the supreme commander of the Allied Forces and later the first supreme commander of NATO.) He understood that war should be an emergency temporary condition, not a permanent one. He understood that humanity must cooperate and be considerate, fair, and just to achieve a lasting peace. I feel that finding our way to peace is ultimately finding our way to survival as a species. As I have said earlier, humans flourished throughout the millennia not by having superior teeth, claws, muscles, or speed, but rather by utilizing adaptation, civility towards one another, and especially cooperation.

"Beware of the military industrial complex."

From the former supreme commander of the military, it must have been perplexing to hear the President give this warning during his farewell address in 1961. It seems to me that if a guy in that position is warning you about something, it must be pretty serious. But what does it really mean? In July 2024 Google said it means this: "We must guard against the acquisition of unwarranted influence, whether sought or unsought, by the military-industrial complex. The potential for the disastrous rise of misplaced power exists and will persist." In my opinion, the rise of misplaced power happened long ago, not just power in the hands of defense contractors but also in the traditional media, social media, college administrators, pharmaceutical companies, and individual billionaires. One of the largest portions of the annual federal budget is defense spending at over $800 billion per year. If any of the money that is used to purchase weapons of war ends up in the hands of the people who decide whether or not to conduct war, that is an obvious conflict of interest.

"In holding scientific discovery in respect, as we should, we must also be alert to the equal and opposite danger that public policy could itself become the captive of a scientific-technological elite."

Are sophisticated A.I. models managing the stream of data coming at us already? Are those models molding our understanding of the world and influencing the individuals who make public policy and the individuals who vote? The answer is clear if you pay attention. What is amazing to me is how far some of our ancestors could see into the future.

T.S. Eliot
American-English poet, playwright, author, editor, and a leader of the Modernist movement in poetry. 1888 to 1965

"Only those who will risk going too far can possibly find out how far one can go."

The path to greatness almost always involves risk, and there is certainly too much risk aversion in the world today. While some risks, such as personal injury, can be reckless, a lot of "risks" are really self-imposed limitations – the risk of shame, embarrassment, failure, starting over, etc. Shrug those off and try a new path. How far can you go?

"Humankind cannot bear very much reality."

It's hard to think about your own death, the death of your loved ones, the evils that men do, how brief our time on earth is, how fragile each life is, the distance between habitable planets, and the odds that our species will continue forever. Now, stop thinking about all of that because you've been blessed with one life to live and need to go out and make the most of each day of that life.

"Some editors are failed writers, but so are most writers."

Funny. Somewhere around ninety-nine percent of books don't cover the cost to produce them. It's a very difficult thing to discover what exactly will strike people's fancy and catch fire. Hence, don't write something unless you are totally comfortable with the likelihood that no one will ever read it or care that it was written.

Ralph Waldo Emerson
American essayist, lecturer, philosopher, abolitionist, and poet who led the transcendentalist movement in the mid-1800s. He was seen as a champion of individualism, and his ideology was disseminated through dozens of published essays and public lectures across the United States. 1803 to 1882

"Do not go where the path may lead, go instead where there is no path and leave a trail."

I kept this quote on my wall during college, when I was more rebellious. Still today, I think it's good to get comfortable with going your own way. When there is no easy path to get where you're headed, it's okay to go off-road and blaze a new trail (with a machete, if necessary). I have found that when that new, more efficient trail is in place, other folks are happy it's there.

"What lies behind us and what lies before us are tiny matters compared to what lies within us."

Strong people are going to overcome whatever lies in their past and surmount whatever comes in their future. Our character matters, to ourselves and to those around us. How we feel about our own actions matters.

"The only way to have a friend is to be one."

If you have some good friends, you know this is true. Most sane people are not looking for a one-way relationship where they constantly give friendship and receive nothing in return. Long-term friendship has to be a two-way street, like love.

"Some will always be above others. Destroy the inequality today, and it will appear again tomorrow."

Well, I suppose in the era in which we live, this might be the most controversial quote in this book. Even if you made all Americans equal today, they would be unequal by tomorrow. Emerson figured this out close to 200 years ago, and it is still true today. Some people have IQs of 85 and others have IQs of 170. Some people are 5'6" tall and others are 6'10". Some folks can labor 10 hours a day seven days a weeks, and others would not survive that pace. No two of us humans are exactly the same, with the same strengths and weaknesses, assets and liabilities. It's called reality, and accepting it is probably the best path forward. You can take the poker hand you've been dealt and play it to the best of your abilities, or you can sit out of the game and lose by default.

"All life is an experiment. The more experiments you make, the better."

This is good advice if you are an adventurous seeker of truth and knowledge. Go out into the world and experience reality, make mistakes, and discover what works.

"Our greatest glory is not in never failing, but in rising up every time we fail."

This is basically the same thing Confucius said two thousand years before, and a theme you will hear repeated by the greatest minds in history. Most of them did not wake up one day and invent the greatest product, write the greatest book, or build the greatest company. Many of them failed over and over again until they succeeded.

"Nothing astonishes men so much as common sense and plain dealing."

Emerson is obviously joking, but there is some truth to this. Common sense seems in short supply today, and there are many examples to observe. Besides that, we receive a study stream of bait-and-switch ads, worthless coupons, fake notices, phishing emails, and spam calls. Now more than ever, a plain fair deal seems amazing.

"Patience and fortitude conquer all things."

I once engraved this on a rock and gave it to a friend who is like me, in that he tends to lack patience. This is a good quote to remember when your first few tries at a task result in failure. You don't quit. You encourage yourself to apply more patience and more fortitude, more time and more discipline. You try creative problem solving. You attack the problem in endless ways with endless attempts until you overcome it.

"Life is a journey, not a destination."

I have heard my wife say this so many times. It's a good point to remember. A lot of people go through life postponing happiness and fulfillment until some later date, after some goal has been achieved. They think thoughts such as, *Once I have a million dollars, I will be happy,* or *After I retire, I will be happy.* That postponed happiness probably will never happen. You need to find happiness today, if at all possible. Tomorrow may never come, and if it does, it may not be what you expect.

Epictetus

Epictetus was a Greek Stoic philosopher who lived circa 50 AD to 135 AD. He was born into slavery at Hierapolis, Phrygia, which is modern-day Turkey. You might not have heard of him, but he had some strong wisdom to share.

"We have two ears and one mouth so that we can listen twice as much as we speak."

This is good advice, though I will admit that I have trouble following it. When we listen to someone, we need to actually try to understand them, and sincerely caring about what they have to say goes a long way towards understanding. People innately know the difference between being heard and being understood, and if you can understand the other party, you can work together towards real solutions and strengthen real relationships.

"It is impossible for a man to learn what he thinks he already knows."

How many times have you thought you knew something, but you were wrong? I mean you were actually 100% sure of a fact, and you turned out to be dead wrong. Been there, done that. I find it more useful to be 100% sure of nothing. Keep an open mind about everything, at least a little bit, just in case you might be wrong. Sometimes we're wrong a long time, even decades. I don't know about you, but I would rather know the truth and see things correctly, than carry on in an errant delusion.

"All religions must be tolerated... for every man must get to heaven in his own way."

In general, I would agree wholeheartedly with Epictetus that we need to allow all people to worship in their own way. People should find some doctrine or path that gives them peace, comfort, joy, fellowship, faith, hope, love, and all of the other good things that humans are capable of, even if that is being an agnostic or an atheist. However, tolerance can be taken too far. We should not tolerate any religion that forces its beliefs on non-believers, that tries to eliminate other religions, or that kills non-believers as part of its doctrine. That isn't tolerance; it's the opposite.

"God has entrusted me with myself."

The founding fathers of America, such as Thomas Jefferson and John Adams, were students of Greek philosophy, and you can see that coming through in their writings, including the Declaration of Independence, the U.S. Constitution, and the Bill of Rights. They believed that we all have God-given inalienable rights to life, liberty, and the pursuit of happiness, for instance. The statement from Epictetus is something you may want to remind yourself occasionally, or perhaps even remind others if they attempt to control your life.

"If you wish to be a writer, write."

Back in the 1980s, we would have said, "Duh." It seems obvious, yet how many people mope around for decades wishing that they were a traveler, a musician, an artist, a singer, or a builder? All the while, they could have gotten into a car and driven to Canada. They could have bought a guitar and started plucking a string. They could have started singing in a choir. The point of this quote is if you want to be good at something, do it. In fact, I would say do it, and keep doing it, and never give up until you have reached your goals. Does it really even matter how good you get, so long as you are enjoying the journey?

"The reward in a thing well done is to have done it."

Why climb a mountain, paint a picture, or ride a motorcycle across the country? You don't have to do any of those things. The reward is in the doing of the thing. To me, there are a couple of points here. If you are going to do something, do it well, so that you can feel pride in your accomplishment. Secondly, not everything we do has to be done for money or for any reason that is logical to the outside world. Some things are simply a reward for you and no one else. That's okay.

Euripides
Influential and prolific Greek playwright who lived 480BC to
406BC.

"Do not plan for ventures before finishing what's at hand."

> I start with this quote because just last night I was
> lamenting that I have too many open projects. After
> managing a CPA firm that always had dozens of projects
> running at the same time, I know full well that completing
> them sequentially is the most efficient way to progress.
> Trying to do a 10-hour project nine minutes at a time tends
> to turn it into a 20-hour project. More importantly, I know
> that for myself and everyone I've managed, there is a point
> at which you have so many incomplete projects that you
> don't know what to do next. Progress may cease on all
> fronts. Hence, focus, focus, focus on one venture at a time.

"There is just one life for each of us: our own."

> That's all we have, our one life, and it's a one-way trip.
> Don't try to live someone else's life. It isn't for you. Learn
> everything you can from what's behind you, appreciate the
> present, and be hopeful for the future.

"One loyal friend is worth ten thousand relatives."

> I don't know how the friend-to-relative value ratio works
> out for sure, but Euripides certainly puts a high value on a
> loyal friend. I agree with that idea. Even one loyal friend
> can make all of the difference in your life. What if one of
> your loyal friends was Joe Rogan, Oprah Winfrey, or
> Warren Buffet? Would your life be different?

"Prosperity is full of friends."

> I chose this quote because it is an interesting discussion
> point. Those who are prosperous seem to have more
> "friends." Why? Do they have fake friends trying to get
> close to their prosperity? Are they prosperous because of
> the large number of friends helping them? Or, is the sort of

person who likes to obtain wealth also the sort of person who likes to obtain friends? I'm sure you have to look at each case independently for the right answer. I think the inverse is also something to keep in mind. Being too needy does not attract friends. It is more of a friend repellant. Some people feel that they already have enough problems without taking on a new friend with financial difficulties.

"Leave no stone unturned."

You have undoubtedly heard this phrase. Its meaning is pretty simple. When a solution must be found (hiding under some rock somewhere) you leave no stone unturned. You try everything until you find what you are looking for.

Georg Fabricius
German poet, archeologist, and historian who lived during the renaissance. 1516 to 1571

"Death comes to all, but great achievements build a monument which shall endure until the sun grows cold."

We must all face death at some point. Maybe it's easier when you have accomplished what you set out to do with your life. Maybe it's easier to face when you have no regrets and went after great achievements, regardless of success or failure.

Malcolm Forbes
Publisher of Forbes Magazine and former senator from New Jersey. 1919 to 1990

"When in doubt, duck."

It sounds like a joke, but it's actually a good strategy. It works both literally and figuratively. Unfortunately, the City of St. Louis is perennially amongst the top few cities for murder rates. I had a client long ago who was running a housing non-profit in St. Louis. She was inspecting an apartment complex with a few other people when she heard gunfire. A bullet hit her and went through her cheek before they were able to get to the ground. She survived and told me later that everyone around there knows to hit the ground immediately when they hear gunshots. I hope that you never have to live somewhere with random drive-by shootings, but you can apply the lesson figuratively. When you are exposed to any kind of random attack (physically, financially, career-wise), duck first, then figure out the nature of the attack, before you respond.

"Diamonds are nothing more than chunks of coal that stuck to their jobs."

It seems the point is that anyone could transform his or her value in the workplace from a lowly chunk of coal into diamond level by spending the time and effort it takes to become excellent at what he or she does.

"It's so much easier to suggest solutions when you don't know too much about the problem."

Isn't that the truth? I can't tell you how many times I have heard the suggestion, "Just hire more people." Just adding bodies was the never the right solution for me. The moral of this story is that you need to get an actual understanding of a problem in order to suggest real and helpful solutions.

"When what we are is what we want to be, that's happiness."

I can't argue with that. When you have become what you've always wanted to be, you have reached the pinnacle. Try your best to be happy and contented there.

"Too many people overvalue what they are not and undervalue what they are."

It is human nature for most of us to focus on what we do not have and ignore the blessings we do. The same goes for who we are. We all have strengths and skills that we can bring to the table, and if we want to be appreciated for those attributes, we need to have the appropriate confidence in our abilities and self-respect.

Benjamin Franklin

As I mentioned in the prologue, I am a huge fan of Benjamin Franklin, not just for his dissemination of wisdom but for his total body of work. People have written several books about his accomplishments. What he achieved in a lifetime (1706 to 1790) sounds impossible. This quick summary is merely to give you perspective on what kind of man published the quotes that follow.

Young Benjamin started as a newspaper printer apprentice to his elder brother at 12 years old and started writing articles anonymously at 15. He left home with basically nothing at 17 years old, and by 20 he had been to England and back, to work as a printer. He started the Pennsylvania Gazette at 22. I could go on and on, but you can read the details of his life elsewhere. In the interest of time and space, I'm just going to cram the remaining highlights into one paragraph.

As an inventor, Benjamin Franklin invented the lightning rod, bi-focal glasses, and the Franklin wood stove. He created the first volunteer fire department in America and the first lending library. He devised anti-counterfeiting techniques for printing currency. He charted and named the Gulf Stream ocean currents. Franklin helped edit the Declaration of Independence and later convinced the King of France to enter into the Revolutionary War on the side of the colonies, which was critical to winning the war. He established the U.S. Post Office and was the first Postmaster General.

This section is lengthy because Franklin was not just an originator of wisdom, but also a compiler of it. Some of what he repeated was what grandfathers and grandmothers taught grandchildren in the early 1700s by word of mouth. Ben published what he thought was the best of it in Poor Richard's Almanack under the pen name Richard Saunders. Here is some selected wisdom that Benjamin Franklin published in the Almanack over the course of 25 years.

1733

"The poor have little, beggars none, the rich too much, enough not one."

I think his point is that none of us feel like we have "enough" cash or possessions, and some of that distress is just a problem in our own minds. We should strive for more contentment with whatever level of wealth we currently occupy and whatever amount of things we possess.

"To lengthen thy life, lessen thy meals."

This is in the process of being proven 300 years later by way of 21st century longevity research. Fewer calories yields longer life in most studies of mammals.

"He that lies down with dogs shall rise up with fleas."

I probably share this wisdom once a month on average. No matter who you are, you should be very careful about who you spend time with and who you listen to. Try to surround yourself with people who make you better, not worse.

1734

"Would you live with ease, do what you ought and not what you please."

Sorry, but succeeding in life involves some sacrifice and discomfort. Doing what is required is sometimes at odds with personal amusement and leisure time. It may even involve exhaustion and pain.

"No man ever was glorious, who was not laborious."

If you get to know very successful people, you will observe this to be true. If you already are a very successful person, then you know what you've done to get there.

1735

"Keep thy shop and thy shop will keep thee."

Nowadays you could replace "shop" with "business." If you will run your business with diligence, honesty, and discipline, it will likely pay you well in return. My advice to new business owners was generally: "Show up when you said you would. Do what you said you would do. Charge what you said you would charge." If you do those things, I believe you will beat 95% of the competition.

"Three may keep a secret if two of them are dead."

Funny and true. If you actually need a secret kept, tell no one, ever.

1736

"Fish and visitors stink in three days."

Basically, don't overstay your welcome when people graciously allow you to stay with them. You may not be invited back.

"Wealth is not his that has it but his that enjoys it."

This is much more important than it seems. After observing many clients over the years, I always say that 90% of people never obtain great wealth, 8% obtain it without spending it, and only 2% obtain wealth and then enjoy it – which really should be the goal, in my opinion.

"God helps them that help themselves."

Contrary to what many might guess, this is not in the Bible. Benjamin Franklin repeated it, but it actually goes back to an unknown source in ancient Greece.

1737

"Consider then, when you are tempted to buy any unnecessary household stuff, or any superfluous thing, whether you will be willing to pay interest and interest on interest for it as long as you live, and more if it grows worse by using it."

So true today in the materialistic society that we've been living in – a society that readily accepts debt in exchange for disposable products. If you understand compound interest, you will never borrow for frivolous items. Furthermore, anything you spend money on, even without borrowing directly for it, uses money that you could have applied towards some other debt or used for some kind of investment.

1738

"Wish not so much to live long as to live well."

Franklin lived to 84 years old, which was pretty good in the 1700s, and he certainly lived well. Life should not just be surviving, but rather living it to the fullest extent, with love, laughter, travel, adventure, teaching, learning, and making the world a better place.

"Reading makes a full man, meditation a profound man, discourse a clear man."

I think Benjamin is clearly suggesting here that we need to gain knowledge, contemplate life, and discuss what we think we know with others in order to get to the truth.

"Search others for their virtues; thyself for your vices."

In other words, try to notice and focus on the good in other people, while trying to remove the bad habits from your own life.

1740

"Fear not death for the sooner we die, the longer shall we be immortal."

It would be nice to ask Ben more about this one, but he clearly had little fear of death. He and every other signer of the Declaration of Independence was in grave danger of hanging for treason. Maybe he was talking about eternal life in heaven, or maybe he felt that he was well on his way to establishing an enduring spot in history.

"Observe all men; thyself most."

This isn't a new idea, since the sages of Greece recommended to "Know thyself" about 2,000 years earlier. Yet, it's good advice nonetheless. Pay attention to the actions of everyone around you, and especially pay attention to your own actions and your effect on the world.

1742

"Eat for necessity, not pleasure, for lust knows not where necessity ends."

This is a good message for modern Americans. The modern version would be something like "Eat to live; don't live to eat."

"Speak with contempt of none, from slave to king.

This shows how much smarter Franklin was than 99% of us, who speak contempt every day. I wish I would have heard it and internalized it as a child. He knew 300 years ago that nothing good could come from putting out negativity directed at individuals. From slaves to kings, they could easily hear rumors of your contempt, and then respond in damaging known and unknown ways. People may also suspect that if you speak ill of others, you may also be speaking ill of them when they're not around.

"The meanest bee hath and will use a sting."

A bee is tiny and insignificant relative to a human, but they sure can hurt us when they feel threatened. I think Franklin's point here is that you should be careful whom you harm or slander because even someone you deem harmless may retaliate in harmful and effective ways that you don't expect. I'm guilty, too. Sometimes I'm the thoughtless offender, and sometimes I'm the bee.

"Let all men know thee, but no man know thee thoroughly. Men freely ford that see the shallows."

Basically, he is saying that you should not reveal every secret and every weakness you have to one individual. Leave a little bit of mystery out there and a few aces up your sleeve. Certain people you know may turn against you down the road and exploit your vulnerabilities. They may even inadvertently damage you by revealing information that you do not want disclosed to the public.

"Tis easy to frame a good bold resolution, but hard is the task that concerns execution."

I have been working out every week for that last 30 years. I have noticed that every January at the gym, the equipment and locker rooms are filled with people, the New Year's Resolution people. By mid-February, the gym is back to the regular familiar faces, and there's plenty of room to work out.

1743

"Tis easier to keep holidays than commandments."

Everyone remembers to celebrate and enjoy the days of ease. It's the sacrifice and discipline that people tend to forget or overlook.

"A spoonful of honey will catch more flies than a gallon of vinegar."

This is an old saying that I heard a lot as a child, but I'm not sure children hear it much anymore. Basically, if you are sweet and kind, you will be much more likely to get what you want from people, especially people you need to solve a problem for you. It works better than coming at someone with vitriol and anger. It's an easy concept to understand, but sometimes it's hard not to uncork the vinegar in response to perceived injustice or incompetence.

"Make haste slowly."

I have learned over the years that working faster is good up to a point. However, at a certain speed you start to become reckless and error-prone, making more mistakes than progress. You need to find the sweet spot of working with urgency but not so much urgency that you have to redo procedures and correct unnecessary mistakes. Let quality always have a higher priority than speed.

1744

"Drive thy business or it will drive thee."

I've definitely been on the wrong side of this. There were a few times that I felt the public accounting firm I was managing was managing me instead, like I was tied to the top of a raging rodeo bull. It was in control of my time and my actions, rather than the other way around. If you are running a business, be vigilant to maintain control of the business rather than letting customers and situations pull you in directions you should not be going. This can be applied to more situations beyond business. Don't let anyone force you to spend time doing what you should not be doing.

"He who multiplies riches, multiplies cares."

In modern times we would say, "More money, more problems." I think the point is to remind us that the more you possess, the more you have to manage. I will be the first to admit that I have acquired too many possessions in my life. When you get there, you will know. You will look around and say to yourself, "Hey, this stuff has become more of a burden than a blessing." Ironically, with the online ordering of items, it has become harder to get rid of things than to acquire them. So, be judicious about the number of items you allow into your life in the first place.

"A true friend is the best possession."

I truly believe that one good friend can make the difference between life and death. They can correct you when you're wrong, save you when you're in danger, feed you when you're hungry, and even give you a reason to carry on. You can't buy an old friend. You have to earn one, building trust and shared experience over the course of many years. Put in the work to make a true friend, and put in the work to keep one.

1745

"Beware of little expenses. A small leak will sink a great ship."

Some folks have enough "little expenses" to burn up their entire income. Incur enough little expenses, and you will have a big problem.

"A light purse is a heavy curse."

Basically, walking around broke is a hard and often stressful way to live. One study I heard about claimed that 80% of arguments that married couples have are about money. Who knows if that is really true, but I would suspect that it's over half of the arguments. Just think, couples could eliminate a majority of marital arguments by having sufficient savings to not stress about money.

"No gains without pains."

We thought we originated the saying, "No pain no gain" back in the 1980s, but apparently it goes back quite a bit further.

1746

"Dost thou love life? Then do not squander time; for that is the stuff life is made of."

Franklin was keenly aware of spending his time wisely and effectively. Most of us squander some amount of our precious time on earth. (I have certainly watched too many You-Tube videos and played too much computer chess.) We need to focus and re-focus on doing the best we can with the precious time we've been given.

"The sting of a reproach is the truth of it."

It's similar to the saying, "Nothing hurts as bad as the truth." When someone is accusing you of an offense for which you are innocent, it may hurt your feelings somewhat due to their mistrust. However, when your actual guilt in a matter is exposed, that hurts worse. You know you're wrong, and now everyone else does, too.

"Take courage mortal. Death can't banish thee out of the universe."

Fundamentally, this is true. Matter and energy are never lost; they are only transformed. Hence, whatever we are, whatever we were, goes on in some form somehow.

1747

"He that won't be counseled can't be helped."

If you won't listen to anyone's advice, then you will go on in error and in ignorance.

"Better is a little with content than much with contention."

Or, you could say it's better to have little and be content
with it, than to have much, coupled with strife in your life.

**"A slip of the foot you may recover, but a slip of the tongue
you may never get over."**

Tripping and falling is generally a much smaller problem
than saying the wrong thing to the wrong person. How
many times have you (and I) spoken a little too quickly and
carelessly and then wished a minute later that we would not
have made that reckless, insensitive statement?

"A mob is a monster – heads enough, but no brains."

We keep learning that lesson over and over again still
today. In the movie *Men in Black*, Tommy Lee Jones
delivers the line, "A person is smart, [but] people are dumb,
panicky, dangerous animals." In other words, a single
person, given sufficient time, can make good decisions and
behave logically. However, a big group of angry people
often becomes illogical, stupid, and out of control.

"The rich must labour to possess their own."

I think it's a reminder to be careful what you wish for,
especially wishing to be rich. Being rich is not just a free-
ride. All of the assets have to be maintained and secured
for as long as you have them. You have to work just to
keep what you have, and the more you have, the harder you
work. (By the way, the British spell labour with a U, and in
the mid-1700s the American colonists were still technically
British.)

1748

"Liberality is not giving much but giving wisely."

Again, it's amazing how advanced Franklin's knowledge of human behavior was already 250 years ago. The quantity of our generosity is not nearly as important as the effectiveness of it.

"Happy is he, who can satisfy his hunger with any food, quench his thirst with any drink, or please his ear with any music."

This is an excellent message about being resilient and learning to be happy with what you have. It's especially important if you travel a lot. The unusual food, new drinks, and different music you are exposed to should be viewed as a blessing, not an annoyance.

1749

"Wise men learn by others' harms."

It's smart to learn from your own mistakes but even smarter to learn from other people's mistakes. While reviewing tax returns, I tried to learn as much as I could from the real world mistakes I saw clients make. I also told the young staffers that they had an opportunity to learn what to do and what not to do if they paid attention to the clients' actions.

"If passion drives, let reason hold the reins."

I think he is encouraging balance. Being passionate about something is awesome. Let it drive you and promote action, but don't let it run too wild and directionless, like a horse without reins.

"Neither trust, nor contend, nor lay wagers, nor lend, and you will have peace until your life's end."

I suppose he is advising us to stay out of stressful transactions. Don't trust people with your assets or argue with people over money. Don't gamble or lend money to anyone if you want more peace in your life.

"If your head is wax, don't walk in the sun."

He could mean that we need to avoid plainly stupid actions
and obvious dangers, especially life-threatening ones. It
could even be more complex. If your brain is weak or you
are gullible, don't tangle with those who are much smarter
than you are.

1750

"Genius without education is like silver in the mine."

If you keep a smart person ignorant of new information,
their intelligence is useless. If you kept the person with the
highest IQ in the world in a windowless closet, they
wouldn't know anything. Hence, useful intelligence must
be the combination of both raw intelligence and experience.

1751

"Tis in the mind all genuine greatness lies."

Don't fool yourself that someone is great at basketball
because they are tall or a great jockey because they are
short. Those physical characteristics were just step number
one. Don't think that someone was a great author or artist
because they were lucky. The source of any person's
greatness is his or her mind, so focus your energy primarily
on improving that.

"Prosperity discovers vice; adversity virtue."

How many lotto winners and famous musicians spin out of
control? How many famous people have committed
suicide or over-dosed? Prosperity has its benefits (and
risks), but adversity has benefits, too. That is where you
get strong, tough, resilient, and self-sufficient.

"Don't judge of men's wealth or piety by their Sunday appearances."

> Amen to that. People say a lot things and put on all kinds of facades. You need to dig deep if you want to pass judgement on someone's wealth or piety – look at tax returns, personal financial statements, credit history, criminal records, and multiple observations of their reactions to moral dilemmas. I can't tell you how many times I have heard, "My neighbor does X on his tax return. Why can't I do it?" Whenever I say, "OK, let's get a copy of his tax return and check it out", that never happens.

"Tis great confidence in a friend to tell him your faults; greater to tell him his."

> No one wants to hear his or her faults, and friends don't want to stress the friendship by pointing them out. However, sometimes we need to go ahead and share our thoughts and concerns about bad behavior and try to put those we care about on the right path.

"Not to oversee workmen is to leave them your purse open."

> This is a lesson I learned the hard way repeatedly in my twenties. It's the same thing as giving someone a signed blank check. Everyone knows that, theoretically, you shouldn't do it, yet many people do it every day.

1752

"A brother may not be a friend, but a friend will always be a brother."

Apparently, Franklin had a high bar for who he would call a "friend," but I agree with the high bar. A true friend should be a permanent "brother or sister" that you have chosen. In my mind, my friends are friends for a lifetime.

1753

"The goodwill of the governed will be starved if not fed by the good deeds of the government."

Historically, a populace will only tolerate a certain level of mistreatment before they revolt, and governments need to be reminded of this periodically.

"The hand, which gave the life, the life sustains."

This seems to me to be another way to say that we need to respect and take care of our parents and grandparents.

"If you would reap praise, you must sow the seeds, gentle words and useful deeds."

I love this theme of humbly earning praise with kindness and hard work, and it even rhymes. In a world full of harsh words and selfish deeds, you will stand out if you follow Franklin's recommendations.

"Ignorance leads men into a party, and shame keeps them from getting out again."

I don't know if he meant a literal party or a figurative one, but it does takes a little time to realize that you're in the wrong situation, and then leaving it is an uncomfortable necessity. In life, you will do well to extricate yourself from destructive parties and bad situations quickly.

"Haste makes waste."

So simple and so profound. In my life I have been pushed up against countless deadlines. As I said earlier, working faster is good to a point. Then after that point, the rewards go downhill. You start making too many errors, and the outcomes devolve into chaos. It's better to focus on working smarter and doing things correctly as the primary goal. Speed should always take a backseat to accuracy and diligence.

"If you have no honey in your pot, have some in your mouth."

This is really curious. I guess he is saying that if you have spent all of your money, hopefully you still have the experience that you paid for. Make good use of your resources, even if it means using them all up. My family thoroughly enjoyed the History Channel series *Alone*. In a particular episode a contestant was sent home by the medical team due to a dangerous level of starvation. As he was being assessed, he said something like, "I have 33 smoked fish available." It was so ironic. He literally had too much fish in the pot and not enough in his mouth.

1754

"Love thy neighbor; yet don't pull down your hedge."

Everyone wants a little privacy, don't they? It's nice to have a sense of separation and security for yourself, regardless of who is on the other side of your hedge.

"Where sense is wanting, everything is wanting."

Basically, if you don't make reasonable decisions, you will have very little. A lack of common sense is going to result in a lack of common comforts most of the time.

"Learning to the studious; riches to the careful; power to the bold; heaven to the virtuous."

It's interesting to ponder the idea that each of us has a different set of strengths and a tailored, unique reward waiting for us if we use those strengths well.

"Were an angelic being to take flight from this part of the universe, and to proceed in a direct course with the swiftness of light, it is certain that, should he continue his flight for all eternity, he must still find himself in the center of the divine presence."

I think this is an elegant way to say that God is omnipresent and eternal.

1755

"When the wine enters, out goes the truth."

So, if you know some information that should not be disclosed, maybe don't get drunk in public.

"If you would be loved, love and be loveable."

So simple and so true. If you want to be loved, love people and be a lovable sort of person. It's a formula we should all remember. To take it further, if you would like to make a friend, you need to sincerely care about that person before you expect them to sincerely care about you. One could say, if you would have a friend, be friendly and be a friend.

"Where there is hunger, law is not regarded; and where law is not regarded, there will be hunger."

Seems like a poignant and useful message for society to remember. Consider the future visualized in the *Mad Max* movies. If we are not vigilant, we can get into a negative feedback loop whereby lawlessness yields despair, and despair yields more lawlessness.

"The doors of wisdom are never shut."

It's hard to say exactly what Franklin was communicating, but here are a few possibilities. 1) Unlike a private country club or ivy league school, wisdom is accessible to anyone. 2) No one has all of the wisdom; hence, there is always more wisdom to learn. 3) Since the world is always changing, and technology is always advancing, the known body of wisdom is always evolving.

"The master's eye will do more work than both his hands."

Someone who has mastered a skill is far more efficient than someone who is still learning. He sees all of the corners that can be cut and avoids all of the pitfalls that will waste time and energy.

"A long life may not be good enough, but a good life is long enough."

I think Franklin is emphasizing here that simply surviving a long time is not necessarily fulfilling. Living well, laughing often, and being loved are more important aspects of life than the length of it.

"Be at war with your vices, at peace with your neighbors, and let every new year find you a better man."

This is a nice toast that I hope to remember. It very much summarizes Franklin's way of life, at least in the early years. He focused every day on improving himself and avoiding vices. He also tried to avoid arguments and angering the people he knew. Rather than aggressively telling people directly that they were wrong, he would ask them a series of questions until they figured out that they were wrong.

1756

"Remember, a patch on your coat and money in your pocket is better and more creditable than a debt on your back and no money to take it off."

Franklin was anti-debt. He believed it was better and less stressful to be poor and debt-free, than to appear to have money by way of borrowing to get it.

"Plough deep while sluggards sleep, and you shall have corn to sell and to keep."

If you are working hard while others are sleeping, you will have plenty.

1757

"He that would catch fish must venture his bait."

Other more direct ways to say this would *be nothing ventured, nothing gained*, or *if you take no risks, you'll have no rewards*.

"The bird that sits is easily shot."

Everyone has heard about the peril of being a sitting duck. Franklin was big on productivity, and this seems like a warning to stay on the move. Keep yourself busy.

"In studying law or physics, or any other art or science by which you propose to get your livelihood, though you find it at first hard, difficult and unpleasing, use diligence, patience and perseverance. The irksomeness of your task will thus diminish daily, and your labor shall finally be crowned with success. You shall go beyond all your competitors, who are careless, idle or superficial in their acquisitions, and be at the head of your profession. Ability will command business, business wealth, and wealth an easy and honorable retirement when age shall require it."

It's a whole life plan in one paragraph.

"Lost time is never found again."

As we get older, we understand more and more the travesty of wasted time. At least for me, these days nothing frustrates me more than someone wasting my time.

"Early to bed, early to rise, makes a man healthy, wealthy, and wise."

This is one of Franklin's most well-known sayings. In the days before electricity, you could definitely get more done in a day by waking with the sun. Now, I don't think it matters too much which wake/sleep cycle you keep, as

long as you maintain a disciplined schedule that is roughly
the same every day and includes all the sleep you need.

"Little strokes fell great oaks."

They knew even three hundred years ago that the key to
achieving a huge task is to break it down into small actions.
When I was young enough to climb mountains, I would
look up at the peak and think that it looked simply too high
to reach. But, I would take several more steps, rest, and
then take several more. After many hours, most of the
time, I found myself at the peak, looking down on the
seemingly impossible mountain below. You may or may
not be able to cut down the great oak tree, but there is
nothing stopping you from taking several whacks at it,
resting, and then taking several more.

"Women and wine, game and deceit, make the wealth small and the wants great."

Apparently it's an old story – the vices that bring men
down. For now, let's just talk about excessive drinking and
gambling. I have known people who have gambled
themselves into poverty. I have also known people who
drank themselves to death, including a very good friend of
mine. The odds of anything good coming from those
excesses are slim and none.

"If you buy what you don't need, eventually you'll be selling what you do."

Quite simply, if you keep wasting your money on trivial
expenses, you will end up selling critical things for your
life, such as tools of your trade, land, or your home.

"When the well's dry, they know the worth of water."

This looks like the forerunner of the saying you have
probably heard many times, "You don't know what you've
got, until it's gone." I propose that you periodically
imagine your life without someone special, without the

conveniences you take for granted, or without an income. We need to remember the worth of water and all of the other beautiful and sustaining elements of our lives.

"Great estates can venture more, but little boats should keep near shore."

Simply, if you have a lot to risk, you can take bigger risks. If you have very little, you better keep your risks to a minimum.

"When you run in debt, you give to another power over your liberty."

To be a debtor means to give some degree of control to the lender. For some people, it almost feels like slavery to work a job they hate out of fear of missing a mortgage payment or a car payment.

"For age and want, save while you may; no morning sun lasts all day."

We have a lot of people financially unprepared for retirement today who need to think about this. The quote is similar to the saying "Make hay while the sun shines." Some folks may just be resigned to the idea of working the rest of their lives. That idea is fine until they reach the point where they actually cannot work due to physical or mental deterioration. Save prudently and invest wisely, just in case you live longer than you expect.

"We can give advice, but we cannot give conduct."

The saying I always heard was, "you can lead a horse to water, but you cannot make him drink." This is a similar idea. Just because you have told, or even shown, someone exactly what to do to succeed does not mean they will follow through with the actions you've presented.

"You may delay, but time will not."

Time is unforgiving. It keeps marching on with or without us. It keeps slipping into the future, and we can't slow it down no matter how hard we try. In fact, it feels to me like the internet age has sped time up by sucking away our free time with infinite (often wasteful) screen activities.

Other quotes from Franklin that did not appear in the Almanack:

"In those wretched countries where a man cannot call his tongue his own, he can scarce call anything his own. Whoever would overthrow the liberty of a nation must begin by subduing the freeness of speech ... Without freedom of thought, there can be no such thing as wisdom, and no such thing as public liberty without freedom of speech, which is the right of every man."

Franklin wrote this at only 16 years old under the pseudonym Silence Dogood. He was apparently a freedom warrior soon after he could think for himself. It's a message we need to hear again in an era where freedom of speech and thought were recently under attack in America and suppressed like we've never seen before.

"An investment in knowledge always pays the best interest."

Franklin was a big proponent of trying to better himself every day. This is a foreign idea to many people, especially those who stopped trying to learn after high school or college. Thankfully, we can get up every day and learn new things that expand our knowledge base, skills, efficiency, or health. The cost is sometimes even FREE, so why not invest in knowledge?

"Be civil to all; sociable to many; familiar with few; friend to one; enemy to none."

Ben was a master at operating in society. He intended to have no enemies and get along with as many people as possible. In this statement is also the idea that you don't want a whole lot of people to know you too well. If the wrong people know everything about you, they may use the information against you someday.

"He that would live in peace and at ease, must not speak all he knows nor judge all he sees."

This statement is a fancy rhyme to state the same concepts in the previous quote. Sometimes you should bite your tongue and reserve your judgement in the interest of peace and harmony in your life.

"Contentment makes poor men rich; discontentment makes rich men poor."

Interesting play on words. Being "rich" is not just having great monetary wealth. To feel rich you also need to possess great contentment. On the flipside, if you are unhappy and discontented, no amount of money is going to make you feel rich.

"Never leave that till tomorrow which you can do today."

You've probably heard this saying or something just like it. Take care of today's problems today, and then you can handle new problems tomorrow.

"Well done is better than well said."

You probably know a few people who talk a lot about what they're going to do and then ultimately do nothing. When I was growing up, this sort of person was labeled "All blow and no go." You did not want to be called that. Better to quietly do great things, than to tell a big story about the great things you could do. I feel that a fundamental tenet of integrity is always doing what you say you will do. I believe it and live it, and it has served me well. Bottom line: if you declare that you are going to do something, you dang well better do it.

"A penny saved is a penny earned."

In other words, saving an extra penny on your expenses is just as good as earning an extra penny in revenue.

"By failing to prepare, you are preparing to fail."

A more modern restatement is "Failing to plan is planning to fail." This seems like a simple concept, yet how many people are walking around today without a plan for anything? I believe you should have multiple goals and multiple plans to achieve them: short-term goals, medium-terms goals, and long-term goals. Write them all down so you don't have to keep all of the details of your plans continuously memorized.

"He that displays too often his wife and his wallet is in danger of having both of them borrowed."

It's a little bit crass, but funny. There is a bit of wisdom here, too. You may not want to display all of your most valuable possessions, especially to the random public. If thieves don't know what you have, they don't know what you have to steal.

"Honesty is the best policy."

I think that is generally true. If nothing else, you don't have to walk around trying to remember which lies you have told to which associates. But seriously, you will have better long-term relationships with friends, family, and business associates if they find you to be honest, trustworthy, and possessing integrity.

"How few there are who have courage enough to own their faults, or resolution enough to mend them."

If you want to have that integrity I just mentioned, you need to confront reality and recognize your faults. You need to freely admit your mistakes and weaknesses, and follow that up with the work it takes to correct your mistakes and improve your faults.

"Life's Tragedy is that we get old too soon and wise too late."

It's sadly true, but with this book, you have a chance to get wise a little sooner.

"Many people die at twenty five and aren't buried until they are seventy five."

I think Franklin's point is that many people stop dreaming, creating, and exploring early in life, and drift into a mode of simply existing or surviving. That's not really living in Ben's opinion (or mine).

"Rebellion against tyrants is obedience to God."

This statement could have been penned by Thomas Jefferson instead of Franklin. It was proposed to be included on the Great Seal of the United States but was not. It was a justification back at the beginning of this country to break the laws of Great Britain in pursuit of all of the freedoms we enjoy today.

"There is no kind of dishonesty into which otherwise good people more easily and frequently fall than that of defrauding the government."

How many people cheat on their taxes? How much in government funds have been stolen? No one knows. The best auditor I ever met always said, "In every city government someone is stealing something; we just have to make sure it is so small that no one will care." When government funds are stolen, the taxpayers at large suffer. So, don't add to the problem. In fact, please oppose corruption, government fraud, and theft whenever you can.

"Time is money."

How many times have you heard this without ever thinking that Ben Franklin could have authored it? My freshman economics teacher taught the concept, and I remember the class still today. The students were up in arms by his suggestion that every hour they spend sitting around watching television, they could be out delivering pizzas instead and making money. He was teaching about opportunity costs.

"Wars are not paid for in wartime, the bill comes later."

Again, we're still learning and re-learning this lesson over 250 years later.

"We must, indeed, all hang together or, most assuredly, we shall all hang separately."

It's a good idea to remember this in the most difficult times: fires, floods, tornados, wars, depressions, and revolution. Humans are strongest when they stick together and help each other. That was our advantage against the predators on the plains of Africa, and cooperation still today provides security against whatever troubles may come.

"Your net worth to the world is usually determined by what remains after your bad habits are subtracted from your good ones."

As an accountant, I especially appreciate this quote. Your assets minus your liabilities is indeed your net worth, both literally and figuratively. Focus on keeping your good habits exceeding your bad ones, or else you might become morally bankrupt.

"When you're finished changing, you're finished"

Funny and true. I saw so much blind opposition to change during my years running a business. Those who were open to change were open to improvement and success. Those closed to change were just taking up space until retirement.

"In this world, nothing is certain except death and taxes."

This is a quote I have heard many times (being in the tax business.) If you want a business that has never-ending demand, think about the tax business or the funeral business. Hospitals and liquor stores are another couple of good candidates. But seriously, this idea is echoed by several other thinkers before and after Franklin. Basically, you can be completely certain about very little in this world – you're going to die, and the government needs revenue.

Milton Friedman
World-famous American economist and Nobel Laureate. Author of *Capital and Freedom* and *Free to Choose*, and advisor to Ronald Reagan. 1912 to 2006

"There's no such thing as a free lunch."

You have very likely heard this many times. The point is that anything that appears to be free probably isn't. For example, if a money manager is charging you one percent of your portfolio (say $10,000), and then they invite you to a "free" luncheon, is that lunch really free? When you get a candy bar at a parade stapled to a local business coupon, is that candy bar free or will you pay later? In the modern internet era, some folks like to say that if a service is "free," then you are the product. It's not a bad idea to always consider why you are getting the free product, service, or lunch. Make sure you are willing to pay the hidden price.

"Inflation is the one form of taxation that can be imposed without legislation."

Inflation is indeed an invisible tax. You don't realize you're paying the tax because the dollars you hold don't change size or denomination. You don't see the two or three percent inflation tax explicitly listed at the bottom of your receipts. However, you can see the increased price of items at the top of your receipts. The people who create the extra money that keeps that inflation going do it quite easily. It's a lot easier than the work you did to earn your dollars, which are being devalued.

"Governments never learn. Only people learn."

Good point; the government actually has no brain. It is the people running the government who need to learn from mistakes and display the courage to change errant policies.

"We have a system that increasingly taxes work and subsidizes non-work."

I won't get into a long political discussion, but it seems that when you tax something, you will get less of it, and when you subsidize something, you tend to get more of it.

Galileo Galilei
One of the most important scientists in history. He was an Italian astronomer, inventor, engineer, physicist, and author. His studies of velocity, gravity, inertia, and planets were critical to the scientists who came after him. 1564 to 1642

"I have never met a man so ignorant that I couldn't learn something from him."

I had not heard this statement until recently, but I absolutely agree with it. It's easy to look at some people or listen to them and think, "This person could not possibly teach me anything." However, that is wrong. If they are alive and communicative, they probably know some things that you don't. Take the opportunity to learn what they are willing to teach you. You might be surprised.

"Who would set a limit to the mind of man? Who would dare assert that we know all there is to be known?"

You have probably met some people who assert that they know just about everything. Even if they don't admit it, their actions suggest it to be true. Those people are stuck in the mud and don't know it. I think we all need to keep a humble and hopeful mindset, such as "There is always more to learn, and we are always capable of learning it."

"In questions of science, the authority of a thousand is not worth the humble reasoning of a single individual."

How many times in history have the masses been wrong? At one time, there were one or two people on Earth who suspected that the Earth was round instead of flat. At one time there were few people who believed that the Earth rotates around the sun rather than the other way around. I think the important point is that we as a species sometimes make discoveries, which void commonly accepted widely held beliefs. And, there are more discoveries to come.

"It is surely harmful to souls to make it a heresy to believe what is proved."

How did Galileo know about "gas-lighting" 400 years ago? I suppose they had their own version of it in his time. Isn't it a shame, and harmful to one's soul, to be forced to believe a lie? We are told today so often not to believe what we see and not to believe our own logic but rather to go along with group-think. To do otherwise these days is to risk everything you hold dear.

Mahatma Gandhi
Mohandas Karamchand Gandhi was an Indian attorney, civil rights activist, and leader of the movement for Indian independence from British rule. 1869 to 1948

"You must be the change you wish to see in the world."

I am a firm believer in modeling the behavior you wish to see in others. The more of us who are good, the more of us will be good, and likewise to the negative side.

"Live as if you were to die tomorrow. Learn as if you were to live forever."

This is a big one. It's easy to become complacent and procrastinate. Think of the things you would do today if you knew you would die tomorrow. You would probably tell a lot of people how much they mean to you. You might seek forgiveness from someone or resolve previously unresolved business affairs. The second part is deeper. To stay sharp, we need to keeping learning every day of our lives, as if we would live forever. When we are 62, we don't know if we'll live to 72, 82, or 102, so why not stay as sharp as possible all the way until the end?

"An eye for an eye leaves the whole world blind."

Mahatma Gandhi was a proponent of non-violence. I believe this statement was his clever message that ever-escalating violent responses leave more and more people injured or dead on both sides. (Consider the large fatality count in the American Civil War.) Gandhi felt it was better for Indians to gain independence and stay alive in the process. It's better for any two parties to solve their differences without bloodshed, if at all possible.

"Strength does not come from physical capacity. It comes from an indomitable will."

Have you ever been in a life or death situation, in which you must hike out, swim out, climb down, or hold your breath to survive? If so, then you understand what Gandhi is talking about. The force of your will becomes more important than your physical capacity. The power of your will can help you survive all sorts of challenges, including difficult relationships, struggles in school, illness, and financial problems.

Arthur Godfrey
American radio and television broadcaster. 1903 to 1983

"Even if you are on the right track, you'll get run over if you just sit there."

In other words, even if you are headed in the right direction, you have to keep moving forward to maintain momentum. Otherwise, you stagnate, and life rolls on without you. Even if you are the best at something, if everyone around you is practicing and working hard to surpass you, they will succeed in time if you don't keep getting better.

<u>Vernon "Lefty" Gomez</u>
American professional baseball player, who won five World Series championships with the Yankees. 1908 to 1989

"It's better to be lucky than good."

You hear this idea repeated frequently. A bit of luck is always welcome. For some of us, luck is the only reason we are still alive. Yet, I feel that luck versus skill is not an either/or scenario. There is no reason you can't be good and lucky. First, make sure you have the skills you'll need, just in case luck doesn't come your way. Then, if you are blessed with luck on top of your hard-fought skills, even better.

"I never had a bad night in my life, but I've had a few bad mornings."

I think this is a good point about consequences. When we're younger, we don't really know what all of the consequences look like (or feel like.) After a fair bit of wisdom acquisition, we start avoiding some "good nights" to avoid the bad mornings that will follow.

<u>Thomas Gray</u>
English poet and professor at Cambridge. 1716 to 1771

"Where ignorance is bliss, 'tis folly to be wise."

It was later shortened to the saying we have all heard, "Ignorance is bliss." This applies to a lot of situations. We don't really want to know certain things, such as the composition of hotdogs, details of our parents' sex life, the worst thing we've accidentally eaten, or the likelihood of the national debt being paid off. When I hear this saying, I sometimes think back to what a smart, young PhD student told me many years ago. He said, "If you are too smart and know too much about the world, you won't get out of bed." Maybe that was true for him at least at that time. There are super-smart folks all over the board with their productivity levels, and there certainly are some who do very little with their intelligence.

<u>Wayne Gretzky</u>
Canadian retired professional hockey player. Probably the greatest hockey player ever, as his nickname was "The Great One." Born 1961.

"You miss 100 percent of the shots you never take."

In my opinion, this is a super-important quote. If you take no shots towards whatever goal you're facing, you certainly will not score. On the flipside, the more shots you take towards a goal, the more of them are going to work. Even with sloppy, bad shots, if you take enough of them, you are eventually going to get lucky and put something into the net. So, why not take a lot of shots?

<u>Edgar A. Guest</u>
British/American poet based in Detroit, MI. 1881 to 1959

"The best of all preachers are the men who live their creeds."

This sentiment is in keeping with many of the great thinkers. Be a living example of the philosophies that you promote. Show the world that you believe what you are saying and that what you are promoting actually works, at least for you.

<u>Forrest Gump</u>
The main character in my favorite movie, *Forrest Gump*. The line was written by the author, Winston Groom, a Vietnam veteran, reporter, and novelist. 1943 to 2020

"Life is like a box of chocolates. You never know what you're gonna get."

You could restate it as "Expect the unexpected." So many people are disappointed or stressed out by the unexpected negative things that happen in their lives. We need to remember that unexpected positive things happen, too. Almost anything might show up tomorrow, so be mentally ready for that possibility. Be ready to struggle against the negatives and also to welcome the positives each day as they come.

Walter Hagen
American professional golfer. 1892 to 1969

"You're only here for a short visit. Don't hurry, don't worry. And, be sure to smell the flowers along the way."

As a person who spends a lot of time hurrying and worrying, I love his sentiment in this quote. I aspire to do better and smell more flowers along the way.

Stephen Hawking
English professor and director of research at Cambridge. Well known author, theoretical physicist, and cosmologist. 1942 to 2018

"One, remember to look up at the stars and not down at your feet. Two, never give up work. Work gives you meaning and purpose, and life is empty without it. Three, if you are lucky enough to find love, remember it is there, and don't throw it away."

There is a lot of wisdom here. First, don't focus on the ground or how small or weak you are; focus on the world, the universe, and the big things you can do. Secondly, I did not learn until about age 52 the value of work to our well-being. I always had plenty of it, so there was no need to think about its usefulness. Upon retiring, I learned that we humans need a good reason to get out of bed and be useful. Our minds and bodies are stronger, healthier, and happier when they're put to a task. Lastly, humans crave love and belonging. It's in our DNA, as tribal animals. For hundreds of thousands of years, we have hunted together, lived together, watched over each other, helped each other grow and build, and buried each other. I agree with Hawking. If you can find someone who truly loves you, cherish them and hang on to that relationship.

"For millions of years, mankind lived just like the animals. Then something happened which unleashed the power of our imagination. We learned to talk, and we learned to listen. Speech has allowed the communication of ideas, enabling human beings to work together to build the impossible. Mankind's greatest achievements have come about by talking, and its greatest failures by not talking. It doesn't have to be like this. Our greatest hopes could become reality in the future. With the technology at our disposal, the possibilities are unbounded. All we need to do is make sure we keep talking."

This emphasis on communication is super-wise. I know there is an enormous amount of political and social division in the world today. However, I have sat across the desk from thousands of people, and 99.9% of the time I have found that we agree on all of the basic important things in life. How can it be that virtually any two people can talk and hear each other and find common goals, but when two mobs of people assemble and start yelling at each other, then there is war? The difference is civil communication. My advice... Keep all lines of communication open with the people you care about (and even the people you don't.) That's how peace in life is maintained, and that's how we achieve great things – talking with each other and working together.

"The universe doesn't allow perfection."

Simple idea, right? However, it is important to remember it frequently to keep yourself grounded in reality, instead of living in a fantasy. I remind clients, coworkers, and business associates often that no one is perfect, including me. I do believe it is noble to strive towards perfection, especially in things that really need perfection, like heart surgery or rocket science, but don't be surprised when perfection is never quite achieved.

"I don't think the human race will survive the next thousand years, unless we spread into space."

I remember having the same somewhat terrifying realization when I was about 10 years old, sitting in the living room of our single-wide mobile home. If humanity will continue in perpetuity, it will have to colonize space at some point.

"There is a fundamental difference between religion, which is based on authority, and science, which is based on observation and reason. Science will win because it works."

I'm going to go way out on a limb here and disagree a little bit. I do not agree that <u>all</u> religion is based on authority or his implication that religion doesn't "work." It has been around for well over 10,000 years, and it would not still exist if it did not "work," per se. I also do not agree that <u>all</u> science is based on observation and reason. During covid times we saw some wishful thinking called "science." Rather, I would propose this. If some religions are open to new ideas and seeking the truth until they find it, and if some scientists are open to new ideas and seeking the truth until they find it, then both of those parties should ultimately end up in the same place many years from now, not in a competition but in total agreement about the fundamental nature of the universe and humanity.

<u>Graham Hancock</u>
British author born in Edinburgh, Scotland who focuses on ancient mysteries. Born 1950.

"While it is often claimed that we live in an era of great freedom, I'm not sure that we do. I think we live in an era of very sophisticated mind control, where propaganda is used to shut down narratives."

We believe we are free to think whatever we want to, which is technically true. The problem is that more and more sophisticated marketing and supercomputers are controlling the messages we are allowed to see and hear.

We can talk to friends and associates, but their stream of data is also being tweaked for maximum profit or maximum political effect. When your view of the "facts" is being manipulated, effectively, your resulting thoughts and conclusions are also being manipulated. I fear that this computerized propaganda machine may get worse as time goes on.

Thich Nhat Hanh
Vietnamese Buddhist monk, author, and teacher. 1926 to 2022

"There is no way to happiness, happiness is the way."

There certainly are no step-by-step instructions to happiness. We need to remember that happiness is not a destination but rather a state of mind. I know it's easy to think of happiness as an end result – something we can get to after graduating, after our internship, after our current job is over, or after we retire. By continuously pushing our happiness out into the future, we can miss years or decades of happiness right here in the present.

Nathaniel Hawthorne
Nineteenth century American novelist and short-story writer. 1804 to 1864

"Every individual has a place to fill in the world and is important in some respect whether he chooses to be so or not."

I would go a step further and say that there is an ideal place for each individual in the world. If you can find the perfect place for yourself, that is where the real magic happens. When you can find a role that is perfectly in sync with your strengths, your interests, and your personality, you will succeed beyond your greatest expectations.

Lisa M Hayes
Modern life coach and blogger.

"Be careful how you talk to yourself because you are listening."

> This is a modern quote but a good point, nonetheless. We probably talk to ourselves more than anyone else. Sometimes in one's life, we are our only fan, our only supporter, our only bodyguard, or even our only reliable friend. In those tough times, we have to maintain faith in ourselves, talk ourselves up, cheer ourselves on, protect ourselves, and give ourselves the strength to carry on.

Frederic Henry Hedge
Nineteenth century New England minister and transcendentalist. 1805 to 1980

"Every man is his own ancestor, and every man his own heir. He devises his own future, and he inherits his own past."

> It's interesting to think about a life in terms of lasting three of four generations. What you do at 15 can affect where you are at 25. The decisions you make at 45 can impact how you are living at 65, and so forth. In my own life, this quote reminds me of some of my thoughts at age 35. At that time, I was a little jealous of my clients who owned inherited farms or acreage in the country. I thought to myself, *How will I inherit a farm?* The answer was, *It isn't going to happen.* So, I decided to roam the countryside and find one to buy. I briefly stepped into the role of ancestor and got my "inherited farm."

Ernest Hemingway
One of the great American authors. 1899 to 1961

**"How did you go bankrupt?"
Two ways. Gradually, then suddenly."**

> He wrote this as character dialogue in the *Sun Also Rises*. It is meant as a joke, but often times the best jokes have a degree of truth in them. In our own lives, once things start down a bad path in a gradual fashion, they can suddenly get far worse. So, turn the tide early on problems in your life.

Give them attention when they are small, so that you don't have to give them attention when they are enormous.

Jim Henson
Henson taught himself to be a puppeteer as a teenager. He created the characters on Sesame street in the 1960s and ran the Muppet Show in the 1970s. He produced several Muppet movies and other ground-breaking films and was considered an artistic genius. He was the voice and mind of the world-famous Kermit the Frog. 1936 to 1990

"I think much of the world has the wrong idea of working. It's one of the good things in life. The feeling of accomplishment is more real and satisfying than finishing a good meal – or looking at one's accumulated wealth."

Jim obviously loved what he did. If you can make a living doing what you love, you have reached life's pinnacle. I imagine it doesn't feel like work at all, more like getting paid to have fun. Not everyone can accomplish this, but it seems like a excellent goal.

"Forget the map. Roll down the windows, and whenever you can, pull over and have a picnic with a pig."

It's so easy to keep driving fast towards a predetermined destination. We tend to miss opportunities to appreciate the here and now, to appreciate the journey along the way. In the end, "now" is the only time we can actually be happy. We can remember happiness in the past and plan for happiness in the future, but we have to actually experience happiness in the here and now.

"I believe in taking a positive attitude toward the world, toward people, and toward my work. I think I'm here for a purpose. I think it's likely that we all are, but I'm only sure about myself. I try to tune myself in to whatever it is that I'm supposed to be, and I try to think of myself as a part of all of us – all mankind and all life.

This is a good message about maintaining a positive attitude and finding what you are supposed to do in life. We are to find our part to play and play it well.

Heraclitus
Heraclitus was a 6th century philosopher from Ephesus circa 535 BC to 475 BC

"No man ever steps in the same river twice, for it's not the same river and he's not the same man."

I think this is a good point about change, in nature and in ourselves. Just because you could climb a certain mountain or swim across a certain lake five years ago does not mean you can still do so today. On the other hand, you might be able to solve a problem today that you could not a year ago. We are always changing, and the challenges we face are also changing. Factor in a degree of variability (and humility) when you approach any situation.

Napoleon Hill
Author of the book *Think and Grow Rich* (1937), which happens to be the only book I've read three times or more. The book says it has launched a million millionaires, and I don't doubt it. Despite his rough and circuitous path to success, Mr. Hill was an insightful purveyor of wisdom. You will see many quotes from him here. 1883 to 1970

"A goal is a dream with a deadline."

Having a deadline is an important distinction between a goal and dream. Anyone can daydream about all sorts of things they want to accomplish, and they can keep dreaming for months, decades, or a lifetime. However, nothing starts to happen towards the achievement of that dream until you set a date to take action. Beyond that, even if you begin to take action towards a dream, it may languish in various states of completion for years and never come to fruition. If you set a deadline for the completion of your dream (and even share it with others), now the urgency and importance can take hold and motivate you to finish your dream, which has turned into a goal.

"The man who does more than he is paid for will soon be paid for more than he does."

It's an interesting turn of phrase and very clever. At first glance it doesn't make sense, but hidden between the words is a message. If you give your employer and customers more than they expect consistently, eventually you will get promotions and raises. In fact, you may eventually be running the business or owning the business, at which point you will be getting paid for more than what you personally do. I can tell you from first-hand experience that delivering to customers more than they expect is a powerful way to run your business, a great way to retain and add customers.

"Any idea, plan, or purpose may be placed in the mind through repetition of thought."

Just like you would study for a test by repetitive reading, mnemonics, and visualization, an important idea, plan, or purpose to your life sinks in and solidifies in your brain by way of repetition. I would further contend that when a problem seeking a solution is at the forefront of your mind, even your subconscious works on it when you are sleeping.

"The starting point of all achievement is desire. Keep this constantly in mind. Weak desires bring weak results, just as a small fire makes a small amount of heat."

Great achievement normally happens only after hundreds or thousands of hours of work towards a goal. It's very seldom that something great happens accidentally after a few hours of casual labor. It is desire that drives the hard work and long-suffering towards a difficult goal.

"Opportunity often comes disguised in the form of misfortune or temporary defeat."

This is cause for hope when bad things happen. Maybe losing a job is the catalyst that prompts successful self-employment. Maybe losing a girlfriend opens the door for a wife. Maybe the desperate need to repair your car stimulates a new pursuit of rewarding mechanical skills. You never know when and where opportunity is going to arrive. Stay open to it.

"It is literally true that you can succeed best and quickest by helping others succeed."

In terms of management within an organization, I absolutely agree. Don't try to lift yourself up by tearing down those above you and next to you. Lift yourself up by lifting everyone below you. Help them grow and succeed, and your own success will follow automatically.

"Success is good at any age, but the sooner you find it, the longer you will enjoy it."

This is a truth that is self-evident, and it's a good reminder to pursue your dreams as early in life as possible.

"Victory is always possible for the person who refuses to stop fighting."

Again, it seems to me self-evident that if you stop fighting, then you have certainly lost. Those underpaid American colonial soldiers marching around with insufficient uniforms and ammunition (sometimes without even shoes) kept fighting for years in spite of many good reasons to quit. However, after some years the French navy joined the tenacious Americans against the British, and with a little logistical luck, they forced the surrender of the most feared army on Earth and allowed for the birth of a nation.

"When defeat comes, accept it as a signal that your plans are not sound, rebuild those plans, and set sail once more toward your coveted goal."

In other words, never let one defeat cause you to give up permanently. Learn from it, change your strategy, and give it another try.

"A positive mind finds a way it can be done; A negative mind looks for all the ways it can't be done."

You probably know some people who immediately list all the reasons something can't be done. I certainly do. It's fine. You just have to ignore them and prove them wrong.

"The way of success is the way of continuous pursuit of knowledge."

I think Charlie Munger (of Berkshire Hathaway) would have agreed with this. Even into his late 90s he stressed that we can and should continue to learn new things.

"Deliberately seek the company of people who influence you to think and act on building the life you desire."

Surrounding yourself with de-motivators is not going to get you anywhere good. I remember a college roommate of mine from Ft. Lauderdale, Florida. His parents weren't wealthy, but he said he hung around with rich kids growing up and learned how they lived and how they thought. He witnessed others living the life he wanted. He got motivated to become an engineer and succeeded quite well in that career, living the life he desired.

"You are the master of your destiny. You can influence, direct, and control your own environment. You can make your life what you want it to be."

I would rather say you can make your life what you want it to be, within reason. If you are 5'5" tall and already 35 years old, you are not going to be an NBA player, but there is no reason you can't go down a path towards owning an NBA team.

"The ladder of success is never crowded at the top."

By definition, there is only room for a small number of people to be honored and recognized as the best in the their field.

"Think twice before you speak, because your words and influence will plant the seed of either success or failure in the mind of another."

Exuding the perception of success is a component of charisma. People naturally want to follow and be associated with a success. If you are at the stage of life where you care deeply about becoming a success, try to plant the seeds of it in the minds of those who may matter to your future.

"Patience, persistence, and perspiration make an unbeatable combination for success."

It's hard to deny it. This is an uncommon combination of traits today, but it will often get you where you're going. Patience is the hardest part for me. You may have a different weakness, but whatever it is, it's important to recognize it and be vigilant against that weakness bringing you down.

"Plan your work and work your plan."

This is quite a famous and much repeated phrase. It's simple but elegant. You need to both create a plan and also pursue it to completion. Furthermore, if your plan isn't working, change the plan, and then work that new one.

"Procrastination is the bad habit of putting off until the day after tomorrow what should have been done yesterday."

Do you know any big-time procrastinators? I would suspect, yes. If so, when they tell you that they are going do something, do you believe them? Doubtful. If you want people to trust you and believe in you, do what you say you will do, and do it in a timely manner. A large portion of the success of my CPA firm was its responsiveness – always completing audits, tax returns, and bookkeeping on time or faster than expected. Life is short, and procrastination does not help you or anyone else.

"If you cannot do great things, do small things in a great way."

When it comes to business, at least, I do agree that the "devil is in the details." If your server smiles instead of frowns, the table is clean, the menu is clear and easy to understand, the drinks come out quickly, the silverware is clean, they keep your drinks full, and you are warmly invited to come back again, you will likely deem this a great restaurant experience. And, none of those things have anything to do with producing exceptionally good food.

"Keep your mind fixed on what you want in life: not on what you don't want."

Spending time thinking about the million things you don't want is a huge waste of your time. It's better to spend your precious time and mental horsepower focusing on what you do want and what you are trying to accomplish.

"If you do not see great riches in your imagination, you will never see them in your bank balance."

It's easy to think you will never have a million dollars, but if you want that to materialize, your mind needs to at least be open to the possibility. If you are convinced that riches are not possible, you probably won't take any action that would allow for it.

"Whatever your mind can conceive and believe, it can achieve."

This is one of the most repeated lines from *Think and Grow Rich*. Maybe it's true and maybe it is not, but you certainly must conceive and believe in something to at least have a chance to make it real.

<u>Hippocrates</u>
Greek physician and philosopher who is generally considered
the father of medicine. American doctors used to take the
Hippocratic oath. 460 BC to 370 BC

"Art is long, life is short."

It is also sometimes stated in the reverse order. I like to
remember it as, "Life is short, but art is long." Interesting
that a doctor was talking about the brevity of human life
and the enduring nature of great art. Even 2,400 years ago,
Hippocrates noticed that one's art can live much longer than
one's body. If you are a great artist, you can become
almost immortal by sharing your creativity and skill with
the world. (This assumes the world takes note and finds
your art exceptional, or course.)

"Let food be thy medicine and medicine be thy food."

Hippocrates knew long ago that our food is the key to our
health. With the right food, you may not need other
medicines. Are you eating the food that will heal you, food
that will make you healthier than you otherwise would be?

"Natural forces within us are the true healers of disease."

I'll admit that I don't know much about medicine, but
everything I have read indicates that having your mind
right goes a long way. Giving your body the time and
opportunity to heal is critical, sometimes more important
than the minutes you receive of personal attention from a
doctor.

<u>Lou Holtz</u>
Head football coach at six different colleges and for the New
York Jets. Born 1937.

**"Life is ten percent what happens to you and ninety percent
how you respond to it."**

It's interesting that one of the wisest things ever said was a quote from a football coach. You need to memorize this one and have it ready at all times. It applies to so many situations. You generally cannot control what happens to you, but you sure can control your response to a problem and frame it in the right way. For instance, if you lose a contest or competition of some sort, you could take the stance of, "I'm just a loser; I should never try again." That obviously has long-term negative results. Alternately, you could take the mindset, "I almost won that time. I can't wait to try again, but in the meantime, I'm going to get better and stronger every day." The later mindset should have long-term positive consequences. It's nearly all about the response.

Horace
The Roman Quintus Horatius Flaccus was a well-known and much celebrated poet in his day. 65 BC to 8 BC

"Carpe diem."

Actually the full quote is "Carpe diem, quam minimum credula postero." This is translated literally as, "Pluck the day, trusting as little as possible in the next one." His point is that we should enjoy life while we can. We should make the most of today because we can't be sure of tomorrow.

"Mix a little foolishness with your serious plans."

I love this. People who know me, know me to be a pretty serious fellow, but once in a while I would do a cart-wheel in the lobby of the office, shoot rubber bands, or jump over a chair. Why? Because we should not be serious all the time. There is a reason that plays and movies incorporate comic relief. Taking your yourself too seriously for too long is a recipe for a heart attack or a nervous breakdown.

Elbert Hubbard
American artist, philosopher, and writer. 1856 to 1915

"To avoid criticism, do nothing, say nothing, be nothing."

Hubbard has a good point, right? If you truly want to avoid all criticism, don't dare do anything. You obviously don't want that, but the harsh reality is that the more you attempt to accomplish, the more you open yourself up to the possibility of criticism. As a child I took a lot of criticism to heart, and frankly became numb to it at some point, probably by age 16 or 17. After that, I kind of ignored and rejected criticism for 10 or 15 years. As an older adult now, I view criticism in a more nuanced fashion. I think we need to listen to it, understand it, decide if it makes sense, change our behavior if we should, and reject it if it's wrong.

"Every quarrel begins in nothing and ends in a struggle for supremacy."

I would not agree that EVERY quarrel begins and ends this way, but far too many of them do. Think about road rage incidents and major world conflicts that did not have to happen, such as WWI. I have seen legal fees in divorce cases or business disputes devastate both parties. In other words, both sides lose. Part of maturing and growing in wisdom is wisely determining which battles to fight and which ones to avoid. For some of us it's easy to want to fight them all, but often times the win simply isn't worth the cost.

Kin Hubbard
He was actually named Frank McKinney Hubbard, and he was an American humorist, cartoonist, and journalist. 1868 to 1930

"The safest way to double your money is to fold it over once and put it in your pocket."

This is funny but also kind of true. When you are thinking about the net income of your business or the bottom line of your household budget, a dollar saved is just as good as a dollar earned.

"We'd all like to vote for the best man, but he's never a candidate."

Maybe we should say he is seldom the candidate? We don't get to vote from a pool of every citizen in America for a particular office; we get to vote for those who are willing to run and find the money for expensive campaigns.

"Beauty is only skin-deep, but it's a valuable asset if you're poor or haven't any sense."

I know that everyone would like to believe that looks are irrelevant. You can complain about it or fight against it your whole life, if you wish. However, the hard truth is that looks can be an asset or a liability. As I have said elsewhere in this book, if you are smart, you will play the hand you've been dealt to the best of your ability.

Victor Hugo
Nineteenth century French author of *The Hunchback of Notre Dame* and *Les Miserables*. 1802 to 1885

"There is one thing stronger than all the armies in the world, and that is an idea whose time has come."

Think about all of the ideas whose time came and what happened subsequently. electricity, automobiles, airplanes, telephones, the internet, etc. You cannot stop the momentum of an idea once everyone realizes that they want it and need it.

David Hume
Scottish author, philosopher, historian, and economist.
1711 to 1776

"Truth springs from argument amongst friends."

If you can have a good civil debate with an intelligent friend, you can normally verify your correct views or change your incorrect ones. There isn't enough of this honest debate or "argument" going on today, just a lot of name calling, gas-lighting, propaganda, and canceling each other.

"Nothing is more surprising than the easiness with which the many are governed by the few."

I don't know how many senators or representatives you have ever spoken with, but if you got to know some, I think you would be surprised by how much time they spend raising campaign funds versus time spent in deep contemplation of the best ways to govern. It's probably human nature to trust that those in charge have it all figured out and continuously work hard to maintain the government. The truth is just a little too scary to accept.

"Heaven and hell suppose two distinct species of men, the good and the bad. But the greatest part of mankind float betwixt vice and virtue."

It is absurd to think about people simply as good or evil. We are all composed of good and evil in differing proportions. Even the best among us will occasionally lie, cheat, or steal, and the worst among us will occasionally feed a stray cat or help up someone who has fallen. One of the difficult aspects of preparing tax returns for clients was figuring out early on where they lie on the moral spectrum. Some were so devoid of morality that we were better off without them as clients – too much risk. Others were obsessed with perfect compliance to laws and rules.

Andrew Jackson
Seventh president of the United States and the only president in history to pay off the national debt. He was a hero and general of the war of 1812, especially known for the Battle of New Orleans. Born in 1767, Jackson was a prisoner of war at age 14 during the American Revolution. He survived two duels during his life and carried a bullet in his chest for 39 years, until his death in 1845. There's a lot one could say about Jackson, but if you study his life, you might think, *This seems like a movie with an impossible plot line.*

"One man with courage makes a majority."

Jackson's courage was legendary. You cannot take this quote literally, but his point is that one person with sufficient courage can achieve a lot more than people would expect. For instance, during World War I, on October 8, 1918, Sergeant Alvin York single-handedly killed 25 German soldiers and took 132 prisoners. York basically constituted a "majority" that day.

"Any man worth his salt will stick up for what he believes right, but it takes a slightly better man to acknowledge instantly and without reservation that he is in error."

Who wants to admit to error? Not too many. It's human nature for us to hide our faults and errors. People do not want to be seen as "wrong", especially in public. During my career, I found it much better (though uncomfortable) to admit error as soon as possible. Denying error only delays the solution and the resolution of the problem. It also causes the victim of your error to get angrier than he or she already is. So rise up, own your errors, admit to them, and quickly get to work correcting them.

James
Brother of Jesus, according to the Bible. ca. 10 BC to 62 AD

"Pure religion and undefiled before God and the Father is this: to visit the fatherless and widows in their affliction, and to keep himself unspotted from the world."

It is interesting to me that the King James Version of the Bible mentions the word "religion" only five times, and this verse is the only one attempting to define religion. It seems to me this must be a fundamental definition that we should keep in mind. Do we spend enough of our time and energy helping orphans and widows these days? Probably not.

"What is your life? It is a vapor, that appears for a little while, and then vanishes away."

Our individual lives are certainly short in comparison to humanity, animal life on earth, the solar system, and the universe. We get caught up in a thousand little problems and waste a lot of that delicate vapor on things that are not important. We need to be reminded regularly how short life is and the imperative to spend our precious time wisely.

William James
American philosopher and psychologist. One of the first psychology teachers at Harvard in 1875. 1842 to 1910

"The best use of life is to spend it for something that outlasts life."

This idea is very important to me personally. Most people don't spend much time pondering what they can do that lasts beyond their own lives, but there are things that all of us can do to contribute to the advancement of humanity – things that can "outlast life." We can raise our children and grandchildren well. We can create art, build buildings, grow companies, create new recipes, write down stories, make videos, and so much more.

"Pessimism leads to weakness, optimism to power."

One of the characteristics of charisma is optimism. People want to follow someone with a plan to win. They do not want to follow someone who believes all hope is lost. It's pretty simple when you think about it. If you wish to lead or gain power, bring your optimism and share it.

"When you have to make a choice and don't make it, that is in itself a choice."

Been there, done that. Have you left a form on a table or desk until it's too late to turn it in? Have you saved a coupon or gift card until it expires? We have all effectively made a decision by not making a decision. It's probably not the ideal approach.

"It is our attitude at the beginning of a difficult task which, more than anything else, will affect its successful outcome."

A positive attitude towards the completion of a task is important not only to display confidence to your cohorts but also to keep your own motivation up. If you think you are probably going to fail a task, you probably are.

Thomas Jefferson
Author of the Declaration of Independence, Governor of Virginia, Secretary of State under George Washington, and the third president of the United States. 1743 to 1826

"Honesty is the first chapter in the book of wisdom."

I think Jefferson is saying that you must hear, accept, and speak honesty if you are going to go down the path of gaining wisdom. If dishonesty is your starting point, you are not going to find true wisdom.

"No more good must be attempted than the public can bear [afford]."

Wow, are we still learning this over 200 years later.... with the US National Debt at over 36 trillion dollars?

"Rebellion to tyrants is obedience to God."

That's a strong statement. There is no doubt rebellion is not always bad or evil. Sometimes it is the right thing to do. The question to resolve is: "Who are the tyrants?"

"When angry, count to ten before you speak. If very angry, count to one hundred."

If I could have learned and utilized this early in life, I would have been in fewer fights. Consider this example: you perceive that someone you don't know has seriously wronged you. You could immediately start yelling, cursing, or throwing punches. In my younger years, those two-second emotional responses were the ones that got me into trouble. Alternatively, you could count to 10 or 100, and then calmly start asking questions about what has actually happened and why. Maybe it wasn't them that wronged you, or you weren't wronged on purpose. I suggest, if at all possible, take a minute, an hour, or a day to take the anger out of your strategic response. Put some logic and reason in there between stimulus and response, rather than just reflex reaction. Not every battle needs to be fought immediately, and some do not need to be fought at all.

"Every American who wishes to protect his farm from the ravages of quadrupeds and his country from those of biped invaders should be a gun man. I am a great friend to the manly and healthy exercises of the gun."

Jefferson did not fight as part of the Continental Army during the American Revolution. He was busy in the Virginia House of delegates and being the governor of Virginia, yet he clearly believed that the common armed man was the ultimate protector of his own farm and his country.

"The tree of liberty must be refreshed from time to time with the blood of patriots and tyrants."[1]

What does this mean? To me, he is saying that tyrants will periodically try to control the populace, censor its free speech, limit its movement, and generally suppress its freedom – the precious tree of liberty. When that happens, patriots must fight (and sometimes die) to eliminate the oppressive tyrants.

"I know of no safe depository of the ultimate powers of the society, but the people themselves: and if we think them not enlightened enough to exercise their control with a wholesome discretion, the remedy is not to take it from them, but to inform their discretion by education. This is the true corrective of abuses of constitutional power."

Jefferson was speaking at a meeting related to the establishment of the University of Virginia. I believe he is saying that the people have to be sufficiently educated to exercise proper judgement and self-control in order to run a functional and free society. (Incidentally, I recently read a story that said ACT scores are at a 30-year low.) Are the voters today sufficiently educated to exercise their control with wholesome discretion? You can think about that and answer it yourself.

"If the American people ever allow private banks to control the issue of their currency, first by inflation, then by deflation, the banks will deprive the people of all property until their children wake up homeless on the continent their fathers conquered. The issuing power should be taken from the banks and restored to the people, to whom it properly belongs."

In case you did not know, the US government allowed the Federal Reserve, a central bank, to start issuing dollars in 1914. That dollar has lost 97% of its value through the beginning of 2025. Something that cost one dollar then would cost over $30 now. Do yourself a favor and study the history, power, and purpose of central banks in the world.

"I place economy amongst the first and most important virtues, and public debt as amongst the greatest dangers. We must make our choice between economy and liberty, or profusion and servitude. If we can prevent the government from wasting the labors of the people under the pretense of caring for them, they will be happy."

How do you think Jefferson would feel about 36 trillion dollars of government debt? While some taxpayers are spending four months of their year working to earn the taxes they pay, is their labor being wasted?

"Never spend your money before you have it."

First of all, I absolutely agree with his suggestion.
However, if you have studied Jefferson, you know that he
was kind of notorious for personally over-spending on
things, such as the continuous remodeling of Monticello.
Maybe that's how he learned the lesson well and is
qualified to speak on the subject.

"The government you elect is the government you deserve."

If you think in terms of YOU as the voting population in a
democracy with fair elections, that's right. For better or
worse, 50.1% of the population gets who they want.
Unfortunately, in a lot of the countries in the world today
you can vote for whomever you like, but the winner is predetermined. In those countries, elections are held to give
the populace the illusion of control.

Jesus Christ
Yeshua in his native Aramaic and Hebrew languages. How to
introduce and explain who Jesus was without offending
someone's sensibilities? Impossible. So, I'm going to keep it
simple. He was born in Bethlehem, which was in Judea at the
time of his birth. As an adult, Jesus traveled around Galilee,
Samaria, Judea, and Israel teaching, healing, and preaching. He
has been known as the way, the truth, the light, and the path to
salvation. His teaching and his life are the foundation for
Christianity, which now has well over 2 billion followers
worldwide, at least one-fourth of the world population.
Between 6 and 0 BC to 33 AD

"The greatest among you will be the servant of all."

I remember this quote often when I am doing difficult
things alone. Whenever it seems that you are working
harder than everyone around you, remember this quote, and
quietly tell yourself, "It's alright. I'm serving others and
doing the things that no one else wants to do. Jesus would
approve."

"Let the one among you who is without sin be the first to cast a stone."

Don't we need to think hard about this one in the era of social media shaming, riots, doxing, and cancelling? Then again, there probably are a lot a folks walking around today who figure they are without sin or that evil simply does not exist. Maybe that's why people are still getting stoned to death, both literally and figuratively.

"Do not be anxious about tomorrow, for tomorrow will be anxious for itself. Let the day's own trouble be sufficient for the day."

It is so easy to worry about the future, and I certainly do. There are literally an infinite number of things to worry about. The best you can, try to focus on solving today's problems today, and worry about tomorrow's problems tomorrow. That is not to say, don't do anything to prevent tomorrow's problems. Just don't waste your time worrying about the many problems that may never come.

"To the one who has, more will be given, and from the one who has not, even what [little] he has will be taken away."

I think Jesus was referring to knowledge and understanding. Gaining knowledge and understanding is the path to gaining more of it, but people who put no effort into gaining knowledge will see the little bit they have decline. The concept can also be applied to money. People with an abundance of money often get more, and people with little money often pursue misguided paths and find themselves with less and less. I also like to explain the idea from the perspective of investments and debt. When you have wealth, it compounds exponentially to the upside, but when you have unserviceable debt, it compounds just as fast in the wrong direction.

"For what shall it profit a man, if he gain the whole world, and suffer the loss of his soul?"

There is no amount of money worth being evil to people and then living with that regret and shame. Lying, cheating, and stealing are wrong ways to make money. Take it from an accountant who has met clients across the wealth and ethical spectrum, you do not want to save on your taxes and then be wondering when the IRS is going to show up. There is much more to happiness and fulfillment than profit. Never exchange your soul for profit.

"So I say to you, ask and it will be given to you; search, and you will find; knock, and the door will be opened for you."

So many people do not ask, do not search, and do not knock. What do you think that yields? No help, no solutions, and no one answering the door. So make an effort, ask the questions, and search for the answers. That's the only way you're going to find what you're looking for.

"Blessed are the merciful, for they will be shown mercy."

This has been stated many different ways. What comes around goes around. Live by the sword; die by the sword. It's karma. The world needs more mercy today, but instead we seem to be in a negative feedback loop whereby bad behavior yields more bad behavior. We need to shift back to a world in which the merciful are shown mercy.

"Love one another. As I have loved you, so you must love one another."

It's a variation on the golden rule. Treat others as you would like to be treated – elegant and simple to understand. In my opinion this should be standard parental teaching, but, sadly, not everyone teaches it. Some parents treat their children (and other people's children) worse than they prefer to be treated. Bottom line, you can't argue against more love in the world. Give love if you hope to receive it.

<u>Steve Jobs</u>
One of the two founders of Apple, long-time CEO, and overseer of the launch of the iPhone. 1955 to 2011

"The people who are crazy enough to think they can change the world are the ones who do."

You can find countless examples of how geniuses were ridiculed and scoffed at before their breakthrough successes. I advise you to use the doubters' disdain. Use it to power your innovation and tenacity to succeed.

"Your time is limited, so don't waste it living someone else's life. Don't be trapped by dogma – which is living with the results of other people's thinking. Don't let the noise of others' opinions drown out your own inner voice. And most important, have the courage to follow your heart and intuition."

It's another good message about not wasting our precious time, not being bound by others' expectations, and boldly going your own way.

"Here's to the crazy ones, the misfits, the rebels, the troublemakers, the round pegs in the square holes... the ones who see things differently — they're not fond of rules... You can quote them, disagree with them, glorify or vilify them, but the only thing you can't do is ignore them because they change things... they push the human race forward, and while some may see them as the crazy ones, we see genius."

Jobs is honoring the people deemed "crazy" because they have new thoughts and ways of thinking outside of the norm. Better ideas are always met with, "It's crazy, and it can't be done," yet the inventors like Jobs stay on track nonetheless and think, "Maybe it can be done; let's try."

"The only way to do great work is to love what you do."

When you love what you do, you are going to give it the time and effort required to be great. That may be hundreds or thousands of hours of effort. You won't find anyone who wakes up one morning with greatness, having never put in the time and effort.

"Simple can be harder than complex."

It's counterintuitive but absolutely true. This message resonates strongly with me at this stage of my life. I've inadvertently managed to make my life in retirement too complicated by managing commercial properties, and making it more simple is going to take hard work. The beauty of simplicity is often spoken about by the great thinkers and often overlooked by the masses. Since our time is precious and finite, we need to utilize simplicity to make the most of every day.

Lyndon Baines Johnson
US Representative and Senator from Texas and 36th President of the United States. 1908 to 1973

"We are all fellow passengers on a dot of earth. And each of us, in the span of time, has really only a moment among our companions."

This is something to remind yourself periodically. Our whole life is just a speck in time. If the history of the earth were compared to a 24-hour day, humans showed up here at 11:59pm. Not just is our own time here short, but our whole species has been around only for a short while. Cherish your precious moment in time and get busy.

Samuel Johnson
One of the most important English authors in history, as his works include *A Dictionary of the English Language*. He was an extremely smart fellow and a prolific writer. 1709 to 1784

"Prudence is an attitude that keeps life safe but does not often make it happy."

This trade-off between risk and reward is one that we face over and over again in life. Johnson is correct that if you pursue nothing but prudence, you're going to have quite a boring and possibly unhappy life. However, if you pursue nothing but imprudence, you will likely have a rather short life full of poverty and destruction. I think experience and the resulting wisdom are what eventually helps us figure out which rewards are worth the risk and which ones are not. There is a proper balance for us to discover.

"Great works are performed not by strength but by perseverance."

Those who observe a great work often don't appreciate or understand the enormous perseverance that built it. They weren't there, and they weren't involved, so it's logical. They may even misconstrue it as easy. I think about the home rehab shows on television during the last 20 years. No matter how bad the house is, it gets completed within a one-hour episode. You see the host swing a sledge hammer a couple of times and screw in a few drywall screws. Before long, they are arranging the furniture, and the house is in perfect condition. Sold! Well... It doesn't really work that way. I once spent every extra waking hour for eight months rehabbing a house – sometimes starting at 6am or finishing at midnight. It wasn't quick, easy, or painless. It didn't get done in an hour. I wonder how many people have watched those rehab shows and launched into a rehab project of their own, only to find it much harder than expected or to find the profit not worth the effort.

"Praise, like gold and diamonds, owes its value only to its scarcity."

This is an important point. Gold and diamonds are shiny and sparkly, but you can't do much with jewelry besides look at it or sell it to someone else who will look at it. The value of gold and diamonds is based more on scarcity and perception than utility. Johnson is saying that the value of praise, like gold and diamonds, is also based purely on scarcity and perception. We all crave it naturally and appreciate it, but we need to internally set a limit on how far we are willing to go for simple praise. Getting our ego pumped up is nice for a few minutes or a few hours, but praise's power and value is fleeting from the standpoint of the receiver. More importantly, we need to think about praise from the standpoint of the giver. The more often you praise someone, the less valuable that praise is perceived. Therefore, be judicious and sincere with your praise if you want it to be valuable.

"It is better to live rich than to die rich."

I would absolutely agree with that. However, I would add this question: Why not do both? After watching the behavior of thousands of clients during my career, I came to this assessment. It seems that about 90% of people will not have a great excess of retirement savings. About 8% of them will have more than enough for retirement but not spend it on what they really want, and maybe 2% will have plenty and also enjoy the riches. I have done no official survey; there is nothing scientific to this assessment. I'm just illustrating that it seems darn few people really enjoy their retirement savings the way we might imagine or hope for. If we can save a lot of money, we ought to enjoy it.

"To keep your secret is wisdom, but to expect others to keep it is folly."

You may not like this, but it's true. For some reason, we humans like to share our secrets with others, but the fact remains that if you absolutely need a secret to be kept, never ever share it with anyone. If you don't care whether or not your "secret" is leaked, then share it as you see fit.

"People need to be reminded more often than they need to be instructed."

I heard a pastor say this recently, and it sounds right. How many lessons have you had to learn a few times?

I certainly have had to learn the same ones over and over again, except, "Do not fall off of a roof." I only needed to learn that once. I have seen several people get annoyed when they think they are being taught "something they already know," yet I think it's actually great to be reminded of prior lessons. Repetition helps the lessons sink in and stay there. For instance, you may already know everything in this book, but I hope you are enjoying the reminders nonetheless.

Percy Johnston
Twentieth century African-American poet, playwright, and professor. 1930 to 1993

"It is the height of absurdity to sow little but weeds in the first half of one's lifetime and expect to harvest a valuable crop in the second half."

That's reality. The actions we take as young people have profound effects on the lives we live as older people. Unfortunately, young folks often don't have the experience and judgement they need in order to do the right things in the first half of their lives. We need to provide them, as early as possible, with real wisdom they can internalize and use to plant the seeds for a better future.

Michael Jordan
Six-time NBA champion, probably the best basketball player in history, and the current wealthiest retired athlete by far, with over three billion dollars of net worth. Born 1963.

"The only real limitation is the one you set for yourself."

If you study Jordan's career from the beginning, you'll see him exceeding presumed limits over and over again with hang time, scoring, championships, endorsements, and in business. Don't set limits for yourself, either literally or figuratively. If you believe something is impossible for yourself, it probably is. On the flipside, you have to believe something is possible in your life for you to have any chance of getting it.

Joseph Joubert
French philosopher, teacher, and author who lived from 1754 to 1824.

"He who has imagination and no learning has wings and no feet."

A person with plentiful imagination and no useful practical knowledge is just a dreamer without the skills to put those dreams into motion. It seems there are plenty of dreamers in the world and plenty of doers, too. However, I don't think we see a whole lot of dreamers who are also doers.

Immanuel Kant
Eighteenth century German author and philosopher.
1724 to 1804

"Science is organized knowledge. Wisdom is organized life."

The body of scientific knowledge is vast and ever-growing. Sometimes even "facts" that we are sure of change. Wisdom is universal, eternal, and unchanging. My opinion is that while much time in school is devoted towards learning the body of science, not enough time is spent learning how to live.

Garrison Keillor
Humorist, author, and long-time radio host. Born 1942.

"They say such nice things about people at their funerals that it makes me sad to realize that I'm going to miss mine by just a few days."

This is a good joke but also a sad reality. A few days after you die, a bunch of people you care about are going to show up and spend the day talking about all the good things that you did. They're going to talk about how they loved you and will miss you. You would have loved to see all of those people in the same place at the same time, but you won't be there to see it or hear it. What is the obvious moral to this story? Throw a party for your aging loved ones and invite everyone they know, so they can be there to enjoy it. Make sure they know how you feel about them on this side of eternity.

"When in doubt, look intelligent."

At a CPA firm, clients call and ask all sorts of questions to the first person who picks up the phone. We had to have the same talk with every young staff accountant: "If you are 100% sure of an answer, you may give it. If you are not, do not guess, babble, or BS the client." Guessing and babbling a bad answer does not foster client confidence. By the same token, in any situation, speak when you have something intelligent to say and something useful to add. Otherwise, hush up and listen. At least look intelligent.

Helen Keller
American author, activist, and lecturer. The first deaf and blind person in the United States to earn a bachelor's degree.
1880 to 1968

"Security is mostly a superstition. It does not exist in nature, nor do the children of men as a whole experience it. Avoiding danger is no safer in the long-run than outright exposure. Life is either a daring adventure or nothing."

Just like our sense of control is often an illusion, our sense of security can be an illusion, as well. A few years ago my daughter was minding her own business driving back to college. All of a sudden a maniac was driving 80 miles an hour in the wrong direction on the interstate and heading straight towards her. Thank God she drove off into the median grass and avoided the head-on collision. This is a prime example of how quickly our "security" can evaporate. Go where you want to go, and do what you want to do, while keeping in mind that anywhere you go has some degree of danger. At least a tiny bit of vigilance is always in order.

Jesse Kelly
Former marine, author, and nationally syndicated radio talk-show host. Born 1981.

"We have to deal with reality as it is, not as we want it to be."

> I heard Kelly say this on the radio, and I have had the same thought many times. It seems to me this is a fundamental issue that gets in the way of good problem solving for many folks today. They see reality the way they want to see it, which doesn't really help them get where they need to go. Imagine you were managing a football team, and you thought you were on the opponent's 20 yard line, while you were actually at your own 20 yard line. You would make bad strategic decisions, like trying to kick an impossible field goal. Correctly assessing reality and the problems at hand is the first step towards actual solutions.

John F. Kennedy
U.S. Representative and Senator from Massachusetts, and 35th President. 1917 to 1963

"The cost of freedom is always high, but Americans have always paid it. And one path we shall never choose, and that is the path of surrender or submission."

> I hope Kennedy is correct in his prediction. This population has changed a lot since 1963, but it is still well-armed and fairly stubborn.

"Let us not seek the Republican answer or the Democratic answer, but the right answer. Let us not seek to fix the blame for the past. Let us accept our own responsibility for the future."

> This seems like a good operating procedure for the government but not the path that we follow frequently. Correct answers are not patented by a party. In fact, some solutions to national problems should be self-evident and sought by both parties. To address the second part of

his statement, I think we currently have an unhealthy obsession with re-litigating actions in the distant past and attempting to erase the parts of history we do not like. Lastly, as for the future, we (including the leaders of today) desperately need to take responsibility for the economic future of this country.

"Let every nation know, whether it wishes us well or ill, that we shall pay any price, bear any burden, meet any hardship, support any friend, oppose any foe to assure the survival and the success of liberty."

It's over 60 years later, and America is still the primary protector of liberty in the world.

"Communism has never come to power in a country that was not disrupted by war or corruption, or both."

He makes a good argument for avoiding, if possible, war and corruption, as they can be pathways to communism.

"Ask not what your country can do for you – ask what you can do for your country."

This is probably his most famous quote. The idea sounds so foreign 60 years later. Do you know many people who are asking themselves what they can do for America today? There are far more asking what America can do for them. I hope someday we can get back to a mentality of pride and ownership of America by the common citizens, a mentality that has people thinking about how they can contribute to the common good.

John Maynard Keynes
Famous English economist, author, and important researcher of macroeconomics. 1883 to 1946

"In the long run, we are all dead."

Keynes was talking about government intervention in long-run economic cycles. It's funny but also good to remember

that you need to concern yourself with *your* lifetime.
Buying an investment that's going to pay off 20 years after
you die doesn't help you much. Sometimes the long-run is
just too far off and too unpredictable to really matter.

Soren Kierkegaard
Danish philosopher, theologian, poet, and author.
1813 to 1855

"Life can only be understood backwards; but it must be lived forwards."

Similarly, the same holds true for the stock market, which
is frustrating. You can analyze the heck out of the past and
understand it well, which may give you some insight into
the future. Yet, the actual future for our lives (and the
stock market) remains a mystery.

"Prayer does not change God, but it changes him who prays."

This is a deep concept. I know this may sound radical, but
I believe that prayer has power, even if atheists do it.
When you shut your eyes and pray, you are focusing your
mind, body, and soul on something. When you do it out
loud, you are focusing yourself on it and the people around
you. Your subconscious goes to work, and so does theirs.
If you believe there is a God, you should communicate with
him. If you suspect there isn't, you should pray anyway.
What do you have to lose?

"Don't forget to love yourself."

Indeed, you are one of the folks who desperately needs
your love and care. Normally, no one is going to take
better care of your mind and body than you are, and no one
is going to look out for your best interest as well as you
can. Hence, love yourself first, so that you can share love
with those around you and take better care of them.

"By a continuing process of inflation, government can confiscate, secretly and unobserved, an important part of the wealth of their citizens."

I could write a whole book about this topic alone, but I will keep it simple. Inflation operates like a secret tax. By allowing the value of the currency to decline by various processes, the government allows your purchasing power to decline. Each dollar that you have becomes less valuable without you even writing a check to the IRS. If you don't want to lose money (technically purchasing power), you need to earn a return on investment that beats the level of inflation or somehow set yourself up with a permanently increasing income stream.

Martin Luther King, Jr.
American minister, activist, and civil rights leader. Nobel peace prize winner and follower of non-violence and civil disobedience. 1929 to 1968

"We must develop and maintain the capacity to forgive. He who is devoid of the power to forgive is devoid of the power to love. There is some good in the worst of us and some evil in the best of us. When we discover this, we are less prone to hate our enemies."

That's some good stuff right there. Living life without enemies is a much better way to live. Your enemies don't care if you're out there hating them anyway. It's difficult, but we should develop and exercise our powers of forgiveness. Don't spend your precious time and energy hating someone. Forgive, forgive, forgive, and go find some joy for yourself.

"Darkness cannot drive out darkness; only light can do that. Hate cannot drive out hate; only love can do that."

It is hard for most of us to respond to hatred with kindness. It is easy to understand from afar how escalating negative feedback grows and sometimes culminates in war. Though it's hard to do, we end up better off responding to negativity

with positivity. The next time a maniac driver cuts into
your lane with no signal at 85 MPH, bless him and wish
him well. He may be heading to the emergency room or
may be a volunteer firefighter responding to a fire.

**"The ultimate measure of a man is not where he stands in
moments of comfort and convenience, but where he stands
at times of challenge and controversy."**

You can't tell how well someone is going to hold up under
pressure until you see them under pressure. Some people
haven't been through serious pressure, so they don't even
know themselves. When you find someone battle-tested
and road-ready, that is someone you can follow. When you
find someone who keeps coming back strong every time
they get knocked down, that is a leader worthy of leading.

"The time is always right to do what is right."

Absolutely. You don't have to make up excuses and
concoct elaborate lies when you do the right thing. You
don't have to wallow in regret or shame when you do the
right thing every time. Take pride in the your work and in
your actions, and be an example for others to follow.

Rudyard Kipling
British author and poet and winner of the Nobel Prize in
Literature. 1865 to 1936

**"We're all islands shouting lies to each other across seas of
misunderstanding."**

How did a guy who died in 1936 know about the internet
and social media?

**"For the strength of the Pack is the Wolf, and the strength
of the Wolf is the Pack."**

It's a good message to remember about teamwork. You have an important role to play as part of the team or as part of a family.

"Take everything you like seriously, except yourselves."

I see too many people taking themselves too seriously. That is a recipe for pain and disappointment. Think about the most serious people you know. Do they have any fun?

"The individual has always had to struggle to keep from being overwhelmed by the tribe. To be your own man is hard business. If you try it, you will be lonely often and sometimes frightened. But no price is too high to pay for the privilege of owning yourself."

Pursuing your own path and going against the tribe has become harder than ever. It was difficult enough before the advent of social media platforms, but now when you feel like going against the grain and taking on the world, you pretty much are.

"War is an ill thing, as I surely know. But 'twould be an ill world for weaponless dreamers if evil men were not now and then slain."

Wow, that's a harsh truth. I have frequently pondered, *Wouldn't it be nice if we didn't have to fight against evil?* Then I realize that evil comes at you whenever it wants, and sometimes you must fight it or die.

Christopher Langan
Widely regarded as one of the smartest people in the world. He lives on a horse ranch in northern Missouri and has an estimated IQ of about 200. Born 1952.

"There's no logical connection between being smart and having money."

I have definitely had some wealthy clients without high academic intelligence, but with a lot of common sense and work ethic. On the other side, I'm sure we have all known plenty of intelligent people who are broke. I would tend to agree that just being smart is no predictor of wealth. Some people just aren't motivated by money and don't care to apply their intellect or their effort to wealth acquisition.

"There is nothing to be gained by pretending that academic involvement is necessary, or even always desirable, in the quest for truth and knowledge."

The availability of knowledge and information these days is a beautiful thing – abundant and sometimes even free. You don't have to be working on your PhD to be effectively uncovering hidden truths and seeking new knowledge.

"If we don't fight for our rights, we're going to lose them. It's as simple as that."

Mr. Langan was speaking recently about the globalist push for more control over the common people all over the world. In the post-revolution rush to get the fledgling US government fired up, the founding fathers wrote the incredible US Constitution in 1787. In the following couple of years they realized that there were some fundamental, critical individual rights not spelled out, so they wrote the Bill of Rights in 1789. As a result, we have enjoyed individual freedoms in this country far superior to those of the populations in most of the countries and empires throughout history. If you are a student of history, you know that Chris Langan is correct. Those in power tend to seize more of it unless someone pushes against that increasing control.

Johann Lavater
Nineteenth century Swiss writer, poet, philosopher and theologian. 1741 to 1801

"Never say you know a man until you have divided an inheritance with him."

If you haven't divided an inheritance with anyone, you may not understand what he is talking about. In the course of my career as a CPA, I observed countless estates being distributed to the heirs. I won't get into all of the stories of heirs taking more than their share or taking everything from their siblings, but to sum it up, it can get nasty, unethical, and even illegal. It spells the end of many familial relationships. My advice is to approach these situations with much transparency, sensitivity, and resolve. Maybe just give your kids the special things you want them to have while you're alive and can still receive their gratitude.

Bruce Lee
Born Lee Jun-fan, he was one of the greatest martial artist/actors ever.   1940 to 1973

"I'm not in this world to live up to your expectations, and you're not in this world to live up to mine."

This is another powerful way to say, "You do you, and I'll do me." It's important not to let other people set your goals or define your happiness.

"If you spend too much time thinking about a thing, you will never get it done."

Bruce and I would have gotten along well. I am sort of notorious for being impatient. I'll plan a task for a bit and then go at it, sometimes without thinking about everything that should have been considered. There is a balance to be struck between unstoppable drive and analysis paralysis.

C.S. Lewis
British author, scholar, and theologian. 1898 to 1963

"Integrity is doing the right thing, even when no one is watching."

Integrity is a crucial virtue in a friend or partner, in my
opinion. Those with real integrity do not turn it off and on
like a light switch. Integrity includes honesty and ethics
and doing what you say you will, even when no one is
watching.

**"When the whole world is running towards a cliff, he who is
running in the opposite direction appears to have lost his
mind."**

It's hard not to follow the herd, and it's hard to face the
lemmings' criticism before they jump off the cliff. Once in
a while you may find yourself the sole voice of reason in a
room full of insanity. So be it. Follow your own path,
even if it is in the opposite direction of everyone else.

**"You can't go back and change the beginning, but you can
start where you are and change the ending."**

As someone who started life in a giant trailer park, this is a
poignant quote for me. You may have your own difficult
history that you overcame, too. Regardless, I love the idea
that wherever you are standing today, you can write the
story of the rest of your life and change the ending.

Abraham Lincoln
Successful attorney, Illinois representative, US representative,
16th president of the United States, and author of the famous
Gettysburg Address. 1809 to 1865

**"Give me six hours to chop down a tree, and I will spend
the first four sharpening the axe."**

This is a famous quote of Lincoln's, and it reminds me of
the old saying, "Never bring a knife to a gun fight." In
other words, be prepared for the task at hand. In fact, there
is more to Lincoln's quote. He was stressing that he would
spend twice as long preparing for the task than performing
the task. I will never forget when, as a young teen, I set
about painting something, maybe an air-conditioner
housing. My older brother saw me about to make a mess

and do a bad paint job. He stopped me and said, "Ninety percent of painting is preparation." I have indeed found that to be true over the years. It's not fun, but it's true. We need to spend the time getting prepared and staying sharp, mentally and physically, and be adequately equipped for the tasks ahead. Sometimes it's even 90% preparation and 10% performance.

"America will never be destroyed from the outside. If we falter and lose our freedoms, it will be because we destroyed ourselves."

Wow, reading this is sobering and somber. What would Lincoln think about where America is today?

"I'm a success today because I had a friend who believed in me, and I didn't have the heart to let him down."

Believing in someone, and making sure they know you do, is not insignificant. It can be one of the most significant things you do in life. There are a lot of people out there walking around doubting themselves – sometimes in every way. You can be the spark that ignites them to keep going or to pursue a dream that seemed too difficult. Our ability to lift someone up is tremendous. We don't use it as much as we should, and that includes me.

"Whatever you are, be a good one."

This is a simple yet profound saying. I have seen over the years that anyone who is the best at what they do is well-rewarded. It doesn't matter whether that is carpentry, dentistry, auto-body work, or teaching. The world loves a specialist, and the best people are eventually noticed.

"There are no bad pictures; that's just how your face looks sometimes."

It's easy to blame the camera for giving you a true representation of yourself. Try improving yourself rather than blaming the camera.

"When you reach the end of your rope, tie a knot and hang on."

> Have you been there? Have you gotten down to the point where you don't know what to do next, except to survive another day? Sometimes that's all there is – to hang on for a while longer until your situation improves.

"You can fool some of the people all of the time, and all of the people some of the time, but you cannot fool all of the people all of the time."

> I like to remind people of this quote when I am discussing business ethics. Honesty with clients and business associates is the best policy in the long run. You can lie and cheat for a week or a month or a year, but the truth will be discovered eventually. When it is, your business associates will not trust you, and your clients will fire you. Be straight-up, fair, and honest with people, and they will recognize and appreciate your integrity.

"The best way to predict your future is to create it."

> Some of us are moving through life as though it is just something that happens to us, totally beyond our control. In reality it is a mix of actions and reactions, some of which are within our control and some of which are beyond. We all have some resources we can put to use: a voice, time, energy, and skills. We can passively wait at home for good things to happen, or we can stand up for what is right, true, good, and productive in the world. We can envision and work towards a better future for ourselves, our family, our friends, and our community.

Walter Lippman
Twentieth century American journalist, writer, and political commentator who won the Pulitzer Prize twice. 1889 to 1974

"The final test of a leader is that he leaves behind him in other men the conviction and the will to carry on."

When you think about great leaders, their organizations or movements carried right on forward after they were gone. Think about Confucius, Buddha, Jesus, George Washington, Mahatma Gandhi, Walt Disney, or Steve Jobs. When you surround yourself with the right people, train them well, and inspire them properly, you have passed the "final test" as a leader and left behind the perpetual evidence of your superior leadership.

John Locke
English philosopher, author, and physician.   He was extremely influential to many of the American founding fathers, as well as Voltaire and other thought leaders that followed. 1632 to 1704

"New opinions are always suspected, and usually opposed, without any other reason but because they are not common."

If you have ever tried to implement change in an organization, you have seen this happen. After presenting an entirely new idea, the typical knee-jerk response is, "It's not how we do it, and it won't work." Yet, how do we ever improve any system unless those who manage it will listen to new ideas and be open to change?

"I have always thought the actions of men the best interpreters of their thoughts."

Pay less attention to what people are saying and more attention to what they are doing. We had a little saying that we would repeat in the office when I was managing the CPA firm: "People say a lot of things." As an auditor, you must approach everything that people say with a degree of skepticism. They may be directly lying to protect themselves or someone else. They may be afraid to tell the truth or afraid to admit their ignorance. There are a myriad of reasons why what people say may not be what they actually think. Watch their actions over time to get closer to reality.

"The most precious of all possessions is power over ourselves."

The freedom to pursue our own happiness is something we tend to take for granted in America. Throughout history and in many countries still today citizens did not have and do not have that kind of freedom. If you have ever had large debts and worked for an oppressive employer, then you have some idea of what it's like to lose power over yourself. I imagine those in prison feel about the same way. Try to never let yourself get into some kind of powerless situation.

"Wherever law ends, tyranny begins."

I guess it stands to reason that useful real laws are made by representatives of the people. When the people's laws are no longer respected, observed, and enforced, a tyrant steps in to quell the chaos. In the end, countries are either governed by laws or by tyrants, or they're enduring the chaos of transition between those two conditions.

"With books we stand on the shoulders of giants."

Isn't it incredible that we can read and learn from the greatest minds in history? We don't have to reinvent the airplane or geometry or rediscover the formula for gunpowder. At this point in the progression of humanity, thousands of books are finished every day, and our collective body of knowledge is compounding.

"It is one thing to show a man that he is in an error, and another to put him in possession of the truth."

To me this seems tricky. How do you not only show someone that they are wrong, which will probably anger them, but also get them to see the light and understand the truth? The best strategy I can think of is to let someone know you respect them and will listen to them. Then ask them to engage in a civil discussion that is long enough to come to a mutual agreement, even if that is a mutual agreement to disagree. I'm probably an oddball on this, but I honestly want to learn the truth even if it means I was completely wrong and need to apologize for my ignorance.

Vince Lombardi
Widely considered one of the best National Football League coaches of all time. 1913 to 1970

"Winners never quit, and quitters never win."

I didn't know who said this at the time, but I must have really liked it at 17 years old because I repeated this quote when I spoke at my high school graduation. It's a great thing to remember that, normally, grit and determination are going to be critical to winning at anything in life. The competition out there is vast, and some of them are pretty darned determined.

"Perfection is not attainable, but if we chase perfection we can catch excellence."

In my experience, this idea is correct. The best mindset is to strive for perfection while realizing that absolute perfection is impossible. I used to tell my newer accounting staff that no one wants their tax return 92% correct. They would prefer their tax return 100% correct (perfect); however, they'll probably forgive us if it is 99% (excellent).

Henry Wadsworth Longfellow
Famous 19th century American poet and teacher.
1807 to 1882

"It takes less time to do a thing right than to explain why you did it wrong."

This is similar to the old saying, "If a thing is worth doing, it is worth doing right." If you've worked on a lot of buildings, cars, or machines, you know this is correct. When you fix something poorly, you will be fixing it again

soon. You probably also know that fixing something badly
two or three times ultimately takes longer than fixing it
right the first time. Everyone involved will be happier
when you perform a task correctly – your boss, coworkers,
customers, family, and yourself.

**"If we could read the secret history of our enemies, we
should find in each man's life sorrow and suffering enough
to disarm all hostility."**

I feel this is probably true in most cases. We all have
problems and suffering that few people know about or
understand, which includes our enemies (if we have any.)
If the enemies are rude, mean, and inconsiderate, they've
probably led a hard life – with abuse, neglect, or
substandard parents. Most people are not born evil. At this
stage of my life, when I see a maniac driver cutting me off
or weaving in and out of lanes, I <u>try</u> to think better thoughts
of the individual. Maybe they are rushing to the emergency
room, or they woke up late for an important job interview
or their own wedding. I'll never know the truth about their
condition, so why not stay happier with a better imagining
of the situation?

**"The heights by great men reached and kept
Were not attained by sudden flight,
But they, while their companions slept,
Were toiling upward in the night."**

This is a poetic way to convey the message that great men
and women don't just suddenly fly up to the top of the heap.
They are working (metaphorically hiking up the mountain)
while others are sleeping. A lot of people work less than
40 hours a week, and some are grinding 40 to 60 hours a
week. Then there are those few who are working on
something, mentally or physically, almost every waking
hour and even forfeiting sleep to pursue their passion.

"Into each life some rain must fall." also **"The best thing
one can do when it's raining is to let it rain."**

Poetic and kind of funny. What are you going to do about the rain anyway: curse it, do a dance to stop it, or cast a spell? The point is that some things are just out of our control, and trying to control them is simply a waste of our time. Metaphorically, I think the "rain" is trouble that comes and goes. You can't stop it; you can only ride it out, but it won't last forever.

Ignatius of Loyola
Spanish Catholic priest who founded the Jesuits and eventually became a saint. 1491 to 1556

"Pray as if God will take care of all; act as if all is up to you."

I tend to agree with that strategy. From what I have seen, there is power in prayer and also in action.

"For those who believe, no proof is necessary. For those who disbelieve, no amount of proof is sufficient."

I think it's always good to consider others' perspectives. When it comes to faith, remember that there are those who need no convincing and those who cannot be convinced. There is even a third group, who is unsure of the nature of God and is comfortable with retaining that uncertainty.

Martin Luther
German priest and author primarily responsible for the Protestant Reformation. 1483 to 1546

"The fewer the words, the better the prayer."

I guess Luther liked to keep it simple and get to the point. When listening to a really long prayer, I do reach a point at which my attention and concentration starts to wander off.

"When schools flourish, all flourishes."

It's hard to argue with that logic. The education of the young is a key to the advancement of a society. The wisdom of the elders and the skill of the master craftsmen is lost a little each day due to the unyielding rages of time. Schools should work to transfer that precious wisdom and replenish those skills.

"Beautiful music is the art of the prophets that can calm the agitations of the soul; it is one of the most magnificent and delightful presents God has given us."

What an elegant way to describe the sound of beautiful music. You have probably heard music that gives you chills, makes you weep, makes you jump up and dance, or picks you back up when you're down. The power of music is almost magical.

Niccolo Machiavelli
Machiavelli was an Italian diplomat, who lived from 1469 to 1527. He was a philosopher, historian, and author who wrote about politics. Poor Niccolo has been hung with a reputation for being evil for centuries because he sometimes focused more on getting things done, than on getting things done ethically. That said, he was insightful and realistic and called the world the way he saw it in 15th century Italy. The point of his book *The Prince* was to advise a local prince on how to deal with the populace. I don't agree with everything he said or promoted, but some of his observances are still quite true today.

"Society is a system in which the loser is always wrong."

This is not something for humans to be proud of; it's just a fact of human nature. The leaders of the American revolution succeeded in gaining independence from the British monarchy. Then they provided the fundamental information for the American history books in the decades that followed. If they had all been captured and hanged, British loyalists in the colonies would have written about the failed, treasonous rebel revolt of the 1770s.

"For it is by foreseeing difficulties from afar that they are easily provided against; but awaiting their near approach,

remedies are no longer in time, for the malady has become incurable."

This is a more long-winded way to state what Benjamin Franklin said 250 years later: Failing to prepare is preparing to fail. We all need to be thinking ahead about the most likely problems we will face: retirement, college tuition, broken cars, leaking roofs, power outages, etc. If we work on solutions early, the odds of being ready for problems go way up. We can create more hearty and sophisticated solutions given more time to do so and by devoting our efforts to proactive preparation.

"Whenever the opponents of the new order of things have the opportunity to attack it, they will do it with the zeal of partisans, while the others defend it but feebly."

An aspect of human nature is a natural fear of and resistance to change. What Machiavelli is saying is nuanced. If you are able to push through change to any system, most people will resist it and attack the change mercilessly. If there are any defenders, they won't be resolute in their defense because they're waiting to see if the new system works or if those pushing back against it will win. Positive change needs time to prove its effectiveness, so keep that in mind if you are an agent of change. You will have to sell the change and sell the patience required for people to watch it become effective.

"It is essential for a Prince to possess the goodwill of his people, otherwise he will be utterly without support in time of adversity."

You could also say something like, if you live like a tyrant, you will die like a tyrant. Hence, you should be good to those you govern; you may very well need their loyalty and goodwill in the future. Furthermore, an organization or a country can accomplish greatness if the relationship between the leader and those being led is strong and the admiration goes in both directions.

"The armor of another never suits you entirely."

If you are trying to replace someone in any kind of role, you cannot and should not try to replicate all of their behaviors. What worked for them, given their unique personality, is not necessarily going to work for you. We need to learn from those who are successful and also be ourselves, wearing our own armor.

"The short-sightedness of men leads them to adopt any measure that for the moment seems good, and which does not openly reveal the poison concealed under it."

I think this is another way to say that people are gullible and tend to go for the first, cheapest, or easiest solution that comes their way. They tend to not to dig deep enough into a solution to find the poison hidden within. For example, almost none of us read the fine print in the contracts and usage agreements we sign. Sometimes that's a mistake we learn about the hard way.

"There are two ways of carrying on a contest; the one by law, and the other by force. The first is practiced by men, and the other by animals; and as the first is often insufficient, it becomes necessary to resort to the second."

You and I would like to always settle problems by way of rules, laws, logic, and reason. Unfortunately, that is not how some people operate. There is a crass 18th century proverb that I always remember. It goes, "Force shits on reason's back." Growing up where I did, I watched this metaphor play out many times. I hate that we can't always have peace and always feel safe, but the reality is that sometimes in this life you will have to meet unwanted force with an opposing force, like an animal, as Machiavelli puts it.

"A man who, in all respects, will carry out only his professions of good, will be apt to be ruined among so many who are evil."

As I said, I think most of us would love to never be in a fight or intense argument again. If no one wronged us for the rest of our lives, that would be just fine. However, that's just not reality. Evil will find you whether you like it or not. I sometimes think about the scenario we've seen in movies many times. A good man is sitting in a bar one afternoon minding his own business having one beer. Some huge, filthy criminal walks in with his associates and tells the man, "I don't like the looks of you, so I'm going to kick your ass." The good man says, "I don't fight, and I don't want any trouble." That's fine, but he's going to be injured or possibly die if he doesn't fight back. If he is going to survive, he is going to have to do some bad things to exit the bar. The point here is that sometimes the real world puts you in a scenario you would rather not be in and forces you to do some things you would rather not do. That's life. You do what it takes to survive.

"There is nothing that consumes itself so quickly as liberality; for the very act of using it causes it to lose the faculty of being used."

Think about a drug addict. Someone tries a dose of drug X, and they like the high. After a few trips on X, one dose doesn't do enough, so they do twice as much a few times until that isn't enough either. It takes more and more of the drug to reach the same high; meanwhile the addict is becoming poorer and unhealthier as the dosage keeps increasing. The same concept could apply to many things, including government spending. The more the government hands out, the more people become reliant on the aid. Since the aid is abundant, the prices of everything go up, and the people need more aid to live at the same level. More aid is given, then even more aid is required. This is why a parent must say NO sometimes. They are trying to build a stronger, more independent child rather than a weaker more dependent one.

"Friendships that are won by rewards, and not by greatness and nobility of soul, are not real and cannot be depended upon in times of adversity."

This is the entourage scenario. Have you ever met anyone rich and famous and paid attention to those around them? If so, you would find some hangers-on and moochers. You would find fake friends who are there solely for the free-flowing wine, women, and song. I don't think this is a common problem for the common man, yet it is a good reminder to build real friendships based on love, respect, and honesty if you want them to survive adversity and last forever.

"The best fortress which a prince can possess is the affection of his people."

You could apply the same concept to the management of your underlings at work. The best management policy you can have is to possess the affection of your people. That is not a quick or easy relationship to build, but it is a durable and useful one.

"Such is the order of things that one inconvenience cannot be avoided except at the risk of being exposed to another."

The point here is that if you keep running from one problem, you will likely be facing another one. For instance, if you don't pay some large medical bills, you may find yourself with reduced credit and the inability to get a loan. Now you can't buy a car or a house. We need to deal with our small inconveniences timely and thoroughly, so that they don't turn into large inconveniences.

"It is a common defect of men in fair weather to take no thought of storms.

Some people will do no maintenance to their car until it stops running. They will not exercise or eat right until they are sick. They won't inspect the roof until it's leaking.

That is one way to live, but it's probably not the best way. You may have heard the old saying, "An ounce of prevention is worth a pound of cure." We all need to devote some of our energies towards preparing for the storms before the storms arrive.

Maimonides
Moses Ben Maimon was an influential Jewish rabbi, philosopher, astronomer, and physician who lived in Spain, Morocco, and Egypt. 1138 to 1204

"Do not consider it proof just because it is written in books, for a liar who will deceive with his tongue will not hesitate to do the same with his pen."

We could certainly expand this ancient observation to include what you watch on television and what you see on the internet. Proof of anything these days takes work.

Nelson Mandela
Anti-apartheid activist who served 27 years in prison and was elected as the first black president of South Africa shortly thereafter. 1918 to 2013

"After climbing a great hill, one only finds that there are many more hills to climb."

I once asked my father, who was about 75 at the time, if he finished his work. He told me that the work is never finished. When I heard that, it sounded profoundly disappointing to me. However, that's reality, and we have to get comfortable with it. No matter how many hills we climb, there are more hills to climb.

"It always seems impossible until it's done."

I recognize that this is a repeated theme in this book. A lot of people who did great things remember what the prospects looked like before their own success. They wanted to warn/inform us that the prospects never looked good, but they plowed ahead anyway in spite of that fact.

"One cannot be prepared for something while secretly believing it will not happen."

Keep this little nugget in mind: secretly believing in failure will very likely yield failure. Unfortunately, I was in many fights between ages 10 and 18. To make a long story short, basically I won every fight that I was sure I would win and lost every fight I (secretly) thought I would lose. Hence, I learned a long time ago that what is going on in your mind is critical to success. If you seriously believe you can win, you probably will win. If not, you should probably avoid that fight or struggle of whatever kind.

Abraham Maslow
American psychologist who created the famous *Hierarchy of Needs*, which describes the range of human desires from physiological needs to self-actualization. 1908 to 1970

"If the only tool you have is a hammer, you tend to see every problem as a nail." Or, more simply, **"If all you have is a hammer, everything looks like a nail."**

(This quote is often attributed to Maslow in 1966, but it may go back to the 1800s.) I love the quote because it has multiple meanings and is applicable in so many situations. It's meant to point out that you should not rely exclusively on your favorite tool or perhaps only tool. Your only tool is unlikely to be the best one for the job. In fact, using the wrong tool for the job is not only unproductive but can also be destructive, like the blunt force trauma of a hammer. Envision using a hammer to install a toilet or a light switch; it's just not going to work. Hence, this is an excellent quote to remember when you observe people trying to solve problems in the wrong way. You can also recite this quote to yourself when you find yourself failing over and over again to solve a stubborn problem, once you finally recognize you are using the wrong tool. We all must find new tools and more creative solutions when we don't possess the right ones to solve our problems.

John C. Maxwell
American speaker, pastor, and author who specializes in
leadership. Born 1947.

**"A leader is one who knows the way, goes the way, and
shows the way."**

This is an elegant and efficient way to express the key
points to great leadership. You must have a good vision
and a plan for the path ahead. You must personally follow
the path that you envision, and if you are a great leader, you
will show others how to follow the same path.

Dr. Phil McGraw
Doctor of clinical psychology, author, and long-time host of the
Dr. Phil television show. Born 1950.

**"It's so much easier to tell people what they want to hear
instead of what they need to hear."**

This happens all the time. You want to make your friend or
loved one happy, so you tell them what they want to hear.
That's fine if their shirt is a color you don't really like.
However, it isn't fine if they're gambling too much, have
too much credit card debt, or are about to commit a serious
crime. Sometimes we need to do the hard thing instead of
the easy thing. We need to tell them that we love them, but
we don't agree with some path they're on. Yes, it's scary
and dangerous, but it's a risk that a true friend should take.

**"Don't wait until you're in a crisis to come up with a crisis
plan."**

This is perfectly logical, yet how many people have no
crisis plan? Multiple studies show that over half of
Americans don't have an extra $1,000 for an emergency
expense. There are other forms of "crisis" to be prepared
for as well: natural disaster, employment, relationship,
home security, or personal safety. Take a little time to
come up with some kind of crisis plan – anything would be
better than nothing.

"If you face adversity in life and don't learn from it, it's a penalty. If you learn from it, at least you can consider it tuition."

I'll admit that I made a horrible real estate investment when I was 24. I owned it for seven years and lost over $20K on it. Not only that, but I personally did hard labor on that hundred-year-old brick house for at least six months. That part felt like a penalty. However, it turned into "tuition" and paid off big-time. That was where I learned to do plumbing, electrical work, framing, flooring, door and window installation, tuck-pointing, dry-walling, and roofing. That "tuition" saved me many times its price in the following three decades via saved contractor costs.

"If you let your self-esteem be determined by your critics, you will spend a lot of time sitting life out. You have to decide that everyone doesn't have to like you, understand you, agree with you, or want you to succeed in order for you to be okay.

This is a very important concept to our mental well-being. Do not let anyone else decide how you feel about you, and do not let anyone else destroy your happiness with their negativity.

"If you do nothing, you get nothing. Life rewards action."

Dr. Phil goes on to explain, "No matter the problem, crisis, or challenge, it's not going to resolve itself or get better based on what you intended to do. It will resolve itself or get better based on what you [actually] do." We used to have a receptionist. Frequently, we would ask her if she had done some task that she was responsible for. Normally her answer was that she was just about to do the thing. Of course she was. There is an old saying, "The road to hell is paved with good intentions," meaning you can have all the good intentions you want, but the outcome is going to go south if you do not follow through.

"I have often counseled people to make certain that they have left nothing unsaid and left nothing undone between them and the people they love."

As someone who lost both parents long ago, I understand this well. When a parent or close friend leaves this plane of existence, there are no more answers to your questions. You cannot explain anything, reconcile the relationship, or show the gratitude that you should have. Furthermore, none of us know when our last day might be, so you probably shouldn't wait until the end to have these important conversations with the people you love.

P.B. Medawar
Sir Peter Brian Medawar was a Brazilian-British scientist and author. His work on graft rejection and acquired immune tolerance was fundamental to tissue and organ transplantation. 1915 to 1987

"The human mind treats a new idea the way the body treats a strange protein; it rejects it."

If you have ever been involved with introducing a new process or program at your work, you know this is true. The normal reflex reaction to anything new is, "I don't like it." Hence, it is best to just expect rejection of new things. Given time, maybe weeks or months, we uncover the truth about the viability of new practices in our lives. Is it better or is it worse? We eventually find the answer if we're willing to try new things and be patient.

Menander of Athens
Menander was an ancient Greek comedy writer.
circa 342 BC to 290 BC

"The School of Hard Knocks is an accelerated curriculum."

We have learned this truth; haven't we? The year I spent managing the cheapest apartments in the worst neighborhoods in St. Louis was certainly an accelerated program. I'm sure you have faced your own hard knocks, and considering that you survived them, you probably learned a lot about yourself and the world around you in short order. Hopefully you're stronger now as a result.

Mencius
Important Chinese philosopher and counselor to the rulers of his day. 371 BC to 289 BC

"We live, not as we wish to, but as we can."

I think the point is that it's great to dream of better days to come, but in the mean time make the best of what you have. Live the best life you can given the cards that you've been dealt.

"If the king loves music, there is little wrong in the land."

Well, I suppose this is a commentary on the character of leaders. If your king loves war and conquest, then there will be pain and suffering for the kingdom. If he loves music, then you might have peace, harmony, and joy.

Michelangelo di Lodovico Buonarroti Simoni
Italian painter, sculptor, and architect who lived from 1475 to 1564. Widely considered to be one of the greatest artists of all time.

"Trifles make perfection, and perfection is no trifle."

I like to think of the quote as "It takes a million trivialities to make perfection, but perfection is not trivial." When I first read this quote, it was an "aha moment." Michelangelo was a detail-oriented guy. He understood that the whole work was comprised of thousands of tiny details, which he had the patience to tend to, one by one. Briefly, when I was in graduate school, I worked part-time as a secret shopper. After shopping several businesses anonymously, I realized that my overall impression of any place (as a customer) was comprised of dozens of details:

the flooring, garbage cans, promotional signs, employee behavior, cleanliness, bathrooms, lighting, paint, and many more aspects. Typically, a place had all of the details handled or none of them. Whether it is in your nature or not, we all must remember that it is hundreds or even thousands of details that get us from nothing to something for any project we undertake. I feel that doing a great job with details is what set my firm on a path of high growth and high profits. Actual perfection is impossible, but near-perfection is possible. It's normally well-appreciated and noticed by the public, if not consciously, at least subconsciously.

"Genius is eternal patience."

Similar to the previous quote, Michelangelo was revealing to us one of his secrets to success – eternal or infinite patience. I doubt that he ever slapped some paint on a canvas just to get the project done or left a sculpture 90% complete. Patience is certainly not one of my strengths, but I admire those who have it in abundance. They can achieve true genius by way of applying eternal (or infinite) patience to their goals. It's easy to start a project. The real trick is seeing it through to successful completion. Can you imagine Michelangelo saying, "I'm growing impatient with this ceiling project at the Sistine Chapel. I'm only going to work on it until Friday at 5pm." If something is important enough to us, we should work on it with no deadlines and eternal patience.

"If people knew how hard I worked to get my mastery, it wouldn't seem so wonderful at all."

If they were being honest, most of the top people in their fields worldwide would tell you the same thing. There is a big price to pay to master any skill. The great ones make it look easy, but it's not normally as easy as it seems.

"The greater danger for most of us lies not in setting our aim too high and falling short; but in setting our aim too low, and achieving our mark."

To me this is a message about striving do more than society expects of you or even more than you expect from yourself. Michelangelo was a proponent of aiming high long before the U.S. Air Force adopted the motto.

Bette Midler
Award winning American singer and actress. Born 1945.

"The worst part of success is trying to find someone who is happy for you."

I picked this quote because I think there is an important bit of wisdom in there. When I am judging the quality of a friendship, my number one test is this: Is this person truly happy to see me succeed, and am I truly happy to see him do so? If that is the case, then you have a real friendship. If you are jealous to see a friend succeed or secretly want him or her to fail, you need to re-explore the meaning of friendship or at least reconsider whether or not this person is actually your friend.

Olin Miller
Twentieth century American author and humorist.
1893 to 1972

"To be absolutely certain about something, one must know everything or nothing about it."

Many of us have discovered that some things we were absolutely certain about turned out to be absolutely wrong. After a few crushing defeats to your ego, you should learn to never be 100% certain about anything. Maybe you knew the tax laws perfectly, but they changed yesterday. Maybe everyone on the planet was certain that there was no life anywhere besides Earth, but they were all wrong. I like Miller's take on certainty. To be certain about a thing, you either need to know everything about it (unlikely) or almost nothing about it, and you're fooling yourself (more likely).

"You probably wouldn't worry about what people think of you if you could know how seldom they do."

We tend to worry that other people are watching us and thinking about our actions all the time. Sorry, for the most part, they are not. If they are, how sad for them. They need to find something else to do.

J. Pierpont Morgan
Banker, world-class investor, and founder of JP Morgan & Co. 1837 to 1913

"A man always has two reasons for doing anything – a good reason and the real reason."

The point is that people say a lot of things. It would be nice if everything you were told was the truth, but it isn't. There are a million reasons someone might be lying to you or omitting some relevant details. When negotiating with another party, keep an open mind that maybe everything they are telling you is factual, and maybe it isn't. Dig for the truth; trust and verify.

Christopher Morley
American author, poet, and journalist. 1890 to 1957

"There is only one success – to be able to spend your life in your own way."

This was one of the quotes I had on my wall during college. Obviously, there are many potential successes to achieve, but I think Morley was taking an over-arching lifetime view with this comment. When you someday look back on your life, will you be able to say that you spent it the way you wanted? Do you have a plan for your life, and are you pursuing it? When you look ahead, does it look like you are going to get to where you want to go?

"Big shots are only little shots who keep shooting."

Think about the well-known big shots out there, like Jeff Bezos, Mark Zuckerberg, Bill Gates, and many more.

They were all little shots at one point. They started small, dreamed big, and kept taking action towards those dreams until they were realized.

"Act like you expect to get into the end zone."

I love to think about projects or goals in terms of taking them to the end zone. You don't know for sure what you are going to have to do along the way, but whatever it is you'll keep driving towards the end zone. When you act like you expect to get to the end zone, your own team is emboldened, and they're more inclined to help you get there. When you look like you expect to get to the end zone, your opponents think twice about trying to stop you.

John Muir
Widely regarded as the father of the U.S. national park system. Nineteenth century environmentalist, philosopher, zoologist, author, botanist, and co-founder of the Sierra Club.
1838 to 1914

"The power of imagination makes us infinite."

Muir saw that whatever humans can imagine can eventually be willed into existence. We imagined flying, visiting the moon, the Hoover Dam, the Great Pyramid, and so many other things that seemed insurmountable. We are still imagining new things and building towards them every day.

"Everybody needs beauty as well as bread, places to play in and pray in, where nature may heal and give strength to body and soul."

Muir saw the mountains and valleys as almost an outdoor temple, something required by our souls. We really need time to be in nature, to maintain mental and physical health. The outdoors is where we evolved for a million years. It's where we are meant to be.

"Climb the mountains and get their good tidings."

The first time I climbed a real mountain I looked down on the Cascades in Washington state with a sense of awe. I thought, *Oh, this is the view that makes the hike worth it.* I was hooked on seeing those incredible views and climbed many more mountains in Colorado, Vermont, Hawaii, Maine, St. Lucia, and Peru. For some of us, there is no adventure like summiting a challenging mountain.

Charles Munger
Billionaire partner to Warren Buffet, who lived to almost 100 years old with a razor-sharp intellect. 1924 to 2023

"Wisdom acquisition is a moral duty."

There is so much opportunity for wisdom acquisition in the world today. You owe it to yourself, to your family, to your friends, and in a way, to society to gain at least a minimal level of knowledge and reason. You need wisdom to make decisions, to decide whether or not orders you've been given make sense, to vote, and to support yourself during your lifetime.

"The world is not driven by greed; it's driven by envy."

This is an interesting point. I think he was saying that we don't just want "more." That can't be it because humans have more and more stuff with each passing decade. Rather, humans do not want to have less than their neighbors. They hate the thought of every one around them enjoying a bigger house, newer cars, better furniture, and better vacations.

"You've got to figure out a game where you do have an advantage, and it has to be something that you're deeply interested in."

This is another way to say that you have to find the right place for yourself in the world. The right place for me was being the managing partner of a CPA firm. The right place for you might be any one of a million different situations.

When you get to that right place, your possibilities are
endless.

**"Make friends with smart dead people. Adam Smith,
Darwin, Cicero, Ben Franklin —whoever interests you.
Read their writing. Steal their ideas. They don't need them
anymore."**

Herein lies the point of this whole book. I want you to see
all of these great ideas, all in one place. Use them for your
own benefit and for the benefit of your family and friends.

"Mimicking the herd invites regression to the mean."

Mathematically, this must be true. If you are doing roughly
the same thing as everyone else, you will be getting
roughly the same outcome as the average person. We have
this deep-seated propensity to go ahead and follow the
wandering herd of humans. Furthermore, the herd of
Americans today gets so many things wrong – it's probably
not a herd you should blindly follow. At risk of offending
some people, here is short list of herd bad behaviors:
unpaid credit card debt, spending too much on college,
spending too much on houses, unaffordable cars, expensive
event tickets, gambling, drug-use, and wasted screen time.

**"Whenever you think something or some person is ruining
your life, it's you. A victimization mentality is so
debilitating."**

I guess there is a remote possibility that someone else is
indeed ruining your life. You may happen to be a prisoner
of war, for instance. However, generally, I agree with
Munger on this. If your life is not going well, it is probably
your response to your circumstances, your decisions, your
motivation, your stubbornness, or something else that you
could change.

<u>Edward Murphy</u>
Murphy was an aerospace engineer who popularized the first adage below in the late 1940s, which may have been started by British mathematician, Augustus De Morgan. The following are known as Murphy's Laws. 1918 to 1990

"Anything that can go wrong, will go wrong."

You have very likely heard this many times. If not, welcome to the real world. When you are planning anything or trying to accomplish any goal, be mentally prepared for problems that seem to come out of nowhere. Anticipate potential roadblocks, and think of contingencies and alternate paths to get where you're going. When I started investing in real estate in my twenties, I used to create elaborate cash flow projections to predict how much money I would make. Over time, I found that they were always missing the biggest expense – the unknown. As a result, now I place little faith in projections. There is the return on investment you hope for, and there is the return on investment you will actually get.

"Nothing is as easy as it looks."

I'm an optimistic fellow, but I've learned this adage over and over again. When you see someone doing something cool on television, such as playing the violin, painting a landscape, or rebuilding a car, you may think, "Hey, I could do that." Well, you probably could sometime far in the future, but not today. It's probably much harder than it looks. These people spent years acquiring the knowledge and skills that they possess today, and they have film crews and editors. Most things are nowhere near as easy as they appear, so be prepared to put in the extra effort.

"Everything takes longer than you think it will."

This is a cognitive bias known as the "Planning Fallacy." It's an exaggeration, of course. Some things do take the time you expect or possibly even less. However, for projects you have never done before, it's pretty accurate.

Projects like changing your brakes, making a new recipe, moving a piano, or building a retaining wall will very likely take you longer than you expect. It's good to build in extra time in your budget and maybe even a lot of it. Perhaps double or triple your estimated hours.

Elon Musk
Founder of Tesla, SpaceX, and many other companies. As I write this, he is currently the wealthiest person in the world. Musk is clearly one of the top people alive today at turning dreams into reality. Born 1971.

"When something is important enough, you do it even if the odds are not in your favor."

Think about saving your family from harm. You're going to try to do that no matter the odds. I would suspect that many goals are "important" in Elon's mind. Hence, he tackles them with endless tenacity and creative problem solving.

"I think it's very important to have a feedback loop, where you're constantly thinking about what you've done and how you could be doing it better."

A lot of us become complacent, including me. We become proficient at a task, and that's good enough in our minds. It's hard to keep pushing for improvement, especially for decades on end. Musk is giving us a clue here to his success: never stop trying to do things better.

"The first step is to establish that something is possible; then probability will occur."

For example, Thomas Edison once believed that there must be some kind of little wire or string that will glow for many days without burning into pieces. Over a year later, Edison said that his team tried over 3,000 different filaments before they discovered one that would work for the light bulb. For whatever you are trying to accomplish, establish that it is possible, then go at it repeatedly and creatively until "probability occurs."

"I think it's very important to have a good, positive culture. Culture fit is extremely important. It's like a sports team. If you have a good team, it can win championships."

This is a little more long-winded way to say something that I used to say to my partners when I was running a CPA firm. I said that a good team can achieve anything and a bad team can achieve nothing. And, that was actually how the situation looked to me as the person ultimately responsible for managing the firm's workflow. In fact, even one player acting needy, whiny, and negative could be enough to disrupt everyone else and slow down everyone else's productivity.

"The thing that drives me is that I want to be involved in things that will change the world."

He has certainly been and continues to be involved in world changing activities. Hopefully all of the world changes are for the better. Hopefully his technological innovations benefit humanity in the short run and the long run.

"We have got to build and grow, and we have to understand the nature of this beautiful universe we find ourselves in."

Obviously I don't know Elon, but from the outside looking in, this quote seems to summarize what drives him – always pushing for greater understanding of the universe in both creative and practical ways. Jordan Peterson said of Musk, "If you are the most creative person in a thousand, and you're the most conscientious person in a thousand, you're one person in a million. And, Musk is probably more like one person in a hundred million."

Jawaharlal Nehru
Significant figure in the Indian independence movement and first Prime Minister of India. 1889 to 1964

"We live in a wonderful world that is full of beauty, charm, and adventure. There is no end to the adventures that we can have if only we seek them with our eyes open."

Most people say that they would not want to live forever. However, I believe Nehru is correct about there being no end to the possible adventures to be had in this world. Therefore, I would certainly take the option to live forever, maybe as a 35-year-old.

Reinhold Niebuhr
American theologian, author, and public speaker.
1892 to 1971

"God grant me the serenity to accept the things I cannot change, the courage to change the things I can, and the wisdom to know the difference."

This is known as the Serenity Prayer, and it's one of the most well-known prayers in America. It's elegant and efficient and a great aspiration for all of us. We need to find contentment in regards to problems that are definitely beyond our control. We need to work on correcting the problems that we can correct, and we need enough wisdom to discern which problems are within our power to correct, given our intelligence, skills, and resources.

Isaac Newton
One of the most important scientists in history. He was a 17th and 18th century English mathematician, physicist, astronomer, author, and a theologian as well. He formulated laws of motion and gravitation, made the first calculation of the speed of sound, developed theories on the composition of color, and had too many other accomplishments to name. 1642 to 1726

"Tact is the art of making a point without making an enemy."

This would have been a great concept for me to learn by 10 years old. I could have avoided a lot of visits to the principal's office. Newton was good at tact, and it was one of the most fundamental components of Ben Franklin's personality, as well. Tact is a delicate dance, and I wish I were better at it still today. If you want to advance within any organization, group, or society at large, you need to find a way to make a point, while minimizing the number of enemies you create in the process.

"If I have seen further than others, it is by standing upon the shoulders of giants."

This is a lovely acknowledgement of the ancestors and forerunners whom we often forget. Hundreds of generations before us studied the world and worked to make their lives and our lives easier. They have blazed a path, left a trail, and drafted a map that we can follow.

"What goes up must come down."

Applicable to a lot of things in the world, such as stock prices, volcanic rocks, fame, golf balls, and heart rates.

"To every action there is always an equal and opposite or contrary, reaction"

This is good to remember if you try to get what you want by force. You may get an equal and opposite force coming back at you.

"Live your life as an Exclamation rather than an Explanation"

Explanations tend to be boring, and they could be called "excuses." But, an Exclamation is always exciting.

Friedrich Nietzsche
Nineteenth century German philosopher, scholar, and author.
1844 to 1900

"That which does not kill us makes us stronger."

This a well-known and often repeated phrase. It is not always literally true because sometimes we are indeed permanently damaged or diminished. However, the point of his statement is that the battles that we fight and survive generally make us tougher and smarter. We learn how to fight more effectively for the next round, and we learn means and methods for coping with hard times.

"He who would learn to fly one day must first learn to stand and walk and run and climb and dance; one cannot fly into flying."

This is similar to the old adage, "You must walk before you can run." It's a good reminder that it takes patience to pursue gradual improvement. There is a path up the mountain, and each step towards the peak must be taken. You don't take four steps and then jump 4,000 feet upwards. A lot of excellent achievements in life are the result of setting up many dominoes and then knocking them all down in the correct order.

"He who has a why to live can bear almost any how."

If you have a reason to live, you will find a way to do so.

Chuck Norris
American karate champion, author, and star of films and television for over 50 years. Born 1940.

"A lot of people give up just before they're about to make it. You never know when that next obstacle is going to be the last one."

This is true. You have to keep focusing on the next obstacle and work to clear it. Then refocus on the following one, without losing patience and resolve. One of them will eventually be the last obstacle in your path.

John O'Donohue
Irish poet, author, and priest. 1956 to 2008

"Where you belong is inevitably where you continue to return."

Where do you continue to return? Whether it's logical or not, we tend to want to be in a certain place more than any other place. That place must be home.

"The vision and actions of a prophet visit a great unease on our comfort and complacency."

That's the problem with prophets. We naturally fear change and don't want to hear any hard truths about major changes on the way.

"Music strikes a deep and eternal echo within the human heart. It is only when you become enraptured in great music that you begin to understand how deeply we are reached and nourished by sound."

When music moves you to tears, then you understand the deep power of sound. It reaches us emotionally in a way that pretty much surpasses all other avenues.

"Consumerism and greed are an awful perversion of our longing; they damage our very ability to experience things. They clutter our lives with things we do not need and subvert our sense of priority."

Guilty as charged. I have far too many things, and I find one of the most difficult challenges in my life is that objects show up in my house faster than I can take them out. We Americans need to work on being content with fewer objects and more joy.

"A house can become a little self-enclosed world. Sheltered there, we learn to forget the wild, magnificent universe in which we live."

In retirement I am starting to learn about the enclosed home world and trying to stay connected to the magnificent world outside. As I said earlier, humans evolved outside, and we are meant to be there close to nature.

"Learn to forgive yourself, let the burden go, and walk out into a new path of promise."

Regret and guilt can bog you down to the point that you can't move forward. Unburden yourself, get lighter, and start down a better path.

"When you can forgive, then you are free."

As I've said before, the people who have wronged you are living their own lives without thinking about the damage they've done. At this point, it's only you burning up your own time and energy with thoughts of victimization or vengeance. It took me a long time to realize this paradigm. Though it may be hard to do, forgive and free yourself from the bondage of anger.

"Real power is the persistent courage to be at ease with the unsolved."

There is a human need to find out all of the answers. It took me until probably about 50 years old to decide that we aren't going to find all of the answers, and that's okay.

"You take with you everything that you have been."

We are each an incredibly complicated quilt made up of many patches of material gathered over the course of a lifetime. All that we are today is the end result of all that we have ever been along the way.

William of Ockham
English Franciscan friar and important medieval philosopher. The principle known as Ockham's Razor is attributed to him, though there is no evidence that he explicitly stated it the exact way it is repeated today. 1287 to 1347

"The simplest explanation is usually the best one."

In other words, unless there is a reason to believe that the simplest explanation is wrong, there is usually no need to waste time pondering more complex explanations. The simplest one is probably correct. I think back to 30+ years ago sometimes when I consider the beauty of simplicity. After college, I was constantly driving all over the Chicago metro area as an auditor. I have to admit that I got lost many times. I would think, *There must be a short-cut from A to C without going through B.* Well, just about every time I tried that I would wind up at F, cursing my decision and the fact that I was going to be late now. As a result, I came up with my own version of Ockham's Razor. "If you know a way that works, go that way." You can apply this principle to all sorts of problems in your life.

George Orwell
Author of the incredibly prescient book *1984*, which was written in 1949. 1903 to 1950.

"In a time of deceit, telling the truth is a revolutionary act."

I hate that we keep floating closer and closer to the dystopia that Orwell envisioned in his book. These days some truths seems elusive and even dangerous to repeat.

Cyril Northcote Parkinson
British naval historian, author, and creator of Parkinson's law. 1909 to 1993

"Work expands or contracts to fit the time allotted."

I heard a partner at the CPA firm I worked for in Chicago say this towards the end of a workday in 1993. He added that it was amazing how many people finish projects between 4:45pm and 5pm every day. Somehow no matter how long or short the tasks were that he assigned to the staff, every project seemed to get done at the end of each workday. I have repeated this saying many times in the last 30 years. It's a bit of human nature to keep in mind. We all want to stay busy, not too busy, and we want to finish what we're working on before we go home.

Louis Pasteur
Famous French chemist and microbiologist during the 19th
century. The "Pasteurization Process" is named after him, and
he is one of the fundamental contributors to microbiology,
whose discoveries have saved millions of lives. 1822 to 1895

"Luck favors the prepared mind."

> People who know me have heard me say this a lot.
> However, I do shorten it to, "Luck favors the prepared."
> There are many ways to get prepared and stay prepared:
> mentally, physically, career skills, personal skills, etc. In a
> lot of situations in life when you see someone who appears
> to be quite lucky, they were probably quite prepared. I
> once met an Irishman on a cruise. He told us about all of
> the raffles, radio contests, and mail-in contests he had won.
> Was he extremely lucky? Nope. He admitted to me that he
> spent a tremendous amount of time buying chances to win
> and mailing in contest entrance forms.

Pericles
One could call Pericles the father of democracy. He was a
well-loved leader and fostered the first real democracy in
Athens, Greece, where he led the city between 461 and 429 BC.
495 BC to 429 BC.

**"What you leave behind is not what is engraved on stone
monuments, but what is woven into the lives of others."**

> To me, this reveals someone who wished to leave a good
> and lasting mark on history and knew the best way to
> accomplish it. His memory lived on the hearts and minds
> of the citizens better than engravings on stone monuments.

Jordan Peterson
Canadian clinical psychologist, author, deep thinker, speaker,
and modern thought leader. Born 1962.

"We all bear the world on our shoulders."

It is an interesting idea that we each have an effect on the destiny of the world. Most people I talk to about global affairs say, "I can't do anything about it; I'm just one person." If everyone took that approach, literally no one would try to improve the world. Thankfully, some people are bold enough to talk about it, think about it, and even act to make the world a better place.

"You're always looking for new information in the off chance that somebody who doesn't agree with you will tell you something you couldn't have figured out on your own!

I resemble that remark. I'm always open to listen to anyone's opinion on any topic, in case I might learn something new or realize that I have been wrong all along.

"It is far better to render beings in your care competent than to protect them."

I assume he is mostly referring to children, and I definitely agree that our primary focus as parents should be raising competent, strong, self-reliant individuals. You cannot and will not always be with them. Hence, it's ultimately on them to protect themselves. If possible, teach them how to recognize danger, avoid trouble, and defend themselves.

"Humility is recognition of personal insufficiency and the willingness to learn."

I don't care how hard you strive for perfection, you aren't going to get there. The striving is noble and good, but when you make the inevitable mistakes and bad decisions, that's when you need to bring on the humility. You need to notice your shortcomings, apologize to those who deserve your apologies, and rededicate yourself to improving your weaknesses. I once heard Colin Powell in an interview talking about making mistakes. He said that you need to do three things after a mistake: get mad about it, figure out what went wrong, and then let it go and move on.

Seems right to me. Unfortunately, a lot of people stop at Powell's first step.

"If you think tough men are dangerous, wait until you see what weak men are capable of."

The weak men may have nothing to lose, and worse than that, they may be highly suggestible and willing to meekly follow the orders of evil leaders.

"Don't underestimate the power of vision and direction. These are irresistible forces, able to transform what might appear to be unconquerable obstacles into traversable pathways and expanding opportunities."

Look at what Edison, Ford, Jobs, Musk and many others have envisioned and then achieved. Find your own vision and direction and start identifying obstacles you need to conquer.

"Compare yourself to who you were yesterday, not who someone else is today."

I like the idea of focusing on improving yourself and doing so one day at a time. Comparing yourself to others will likely lead to envy or disappointment – two things that aren't going to make you happier.

"You are important to other people, as much as to yourself. You have some vital role to play in the unfolding destiny of the world. You are, therefore, morally obliged to take care of yourself."

This idea reminds me of Adam Smith's philosophy that looking out for yourself financially actually ends up helping the whole economic system. I don't recall hearing an idea like Peterson's message before, but it makes sense when you think about it. If we can take care of ourselves, we can take care of others. If we have our own life under control, we can accept new responsibilities within our family or our society and handle them well.

"It took untold generations to get you where you are. A little gratitude might be in order."

We tend to blow off the suffering and effort of our ancestors. Yet, we actually owe them so much. Imagine if you had to invent all of the following in a single lifetime: the wheel, wagons, gas stoves, air conditioning, cars, pencils, glass, the computer, radio, television, safe drinking water, and a million other things we take for granted. Without our ancestors, we would be living like animals.

Plato
Plato was a student of Socrates and a teacher of Aristotle in Ancient Greece. He was a critical figure in western philosophy. ca. 425 BC to 348 BC

"Be kind, for everyone you meet is fighting a hard battle."

It was true 2,500 years ago and is still true today. Remember this possibility when you are about to lose your temper with someone who is being rude.

"No one is more hated than he who speaks the truth."

Why is that? The truth exposes lies. If you want to see someone get really mad, watch them have their lies exposed.

Titus Maccius Plautus
Plautus was a successful Roman playwright who wrote some of the earliest comedies. 254 BC to 184 BC

"You have to spend money to make money." Or, consider our more modern statement, **"It takes money to make money."**

This is normally true. It is not something to chafe at or complain about; it's just a fact that we should accept and use to our benefit. If you have no money, you are in a precarious situation on many fronts. The point of this quote is the less money you have, the harder it is to make some, and the more money you have, the easier it gets. To do almost any productive activity you will need proper clothing, tools, equipment, inventory, capital, or space. If you want to stay on the right side of $0, you have to find a way to save some money and spend it wisely to make more. Those powerful laws of compounding will work for you if you can get the snowball rolling in the right direction.

Pliny the Elder
Actually named Gaius Plinius Secundus.   Roman author, philosopher, and military commander in the early Roman empire.   Died in the explosion of Mount Vesuvius in 79 AD. Born circa 23 AD.

"The only certainty is that nothing is certain."

It seems to me that the longer you live, the more you realize how dangerous it is to declare your absolute certainty about anything. You are certain that the bookkeeper would never steal money. You are certain that you won't be fired before retirement age. You are certain that you'll be married to the same person for the rest of your life. Or, you are certain that you'll see the sun come up tomorrow. It's human nature to take the certainty stance but more realistic to leave open the remote possibility that you're wrong. Maybe your city will be covered by a volcanic eruption tomorrow.

Plutarch
Plutarch was a first-century Greek philosopher and also a priest at the temple of Apollo at Delphi. 46 to 119AD

"I don't need a friend who changes when I change and who nods when I nod; my shadow does that much better."

One of the great benefits of having friends is consulting with someone who sees the world differently. They can give you another perspective to ponder when you're making important decisions. This is why the old saying, "Two heads are better than one," has endured.

"Prosperity is no just scale; adversity is the only balance to weigh friends."

I noticed as a teenager, that it's the friendships born in fire and adversity that are the strongest. This is why veterans who fight wars together at 18 or 19 years old frequently remain friends for the rest of their lives. Think about hard times in your own life. Who was there to help you in your darkest hour, and who disappeared?

"Those who aim at great deeds must also suffer greatly."

Surprise, surprise. Difficult things are difficult and normally require a degree of suffering. I have noticed in America that the tolerance for suffering has been steadily declining for at least the last 40 years.

Colin Powell
A four-star general who became the 12th Chairman of the Joint Chiefs of Staff. He spent 35 years in the military and was the first African-American Secretary of State. 1937 to 2021

"All work is honorable. Always do your best because someone is watching."

I would never argue against doing your best, even when no one is watching. If you want to be good at something, then practice being good at that something. Working hard towards achieving excellence is one of the great rewards this life has to offer, and demonstrating that excellence is your proficiency test.

"Never get so close to your position that when your position goes, your ego goes with it."

This is a great message for retired doctors, lawyers, dentists, and professors. Many retirees struggle after retirement or refuse to retire because their whole identity is their profession. "If I'm not a dentist, then who am I?"

After decades of doing one thing and being one thing, people can lose their sense of self that exists outside of that one thing. My opinion is that we all need to understand who we are and feel good about it, regardless of how we happen to be making money at this time.

"Don't be buffaloed by experts and elites. Experts often possess more data than judgment. Elites can become so inbred that they produce hemophiliacs who bleed to death as soon as they are nicked by the real world."

It sounds like Powell has been around the block and mistakenly followed some "expert advice" along the way. He also discovered that elites live in a fantasy world, disconnected from the harsh reality of the real world.

"Never neglect small details, even to the point of being a pest. Moments of stress, confusion, and fatigue are exactly when mistakes happen. And when everyone else's mind is dulled or distracted, the leaders must be doubly vigilant. Always check small things."

I found this to be true in my role as managing partner. Somebody has to be the annoying pest who thinks about all of the small things that no one else is thinking about.

Ayn Rand
Actually Alice O'Connor, she was a Russian-born American author and philosopher. Her well-known works include *The Fountainhead*, *Anthem*, and *Atlas Shrugged*. 1908 to 1982

"Reason is not automatic. Those who deny it cannot be conquered by it."

It's kind of sad and funny when I watch people try to reason with the unreasonable. They think, "Well, surely these people will do what is logical and reasonable…" Not so. Those who make bad decisions for 20 or 30 years will very likely continue to make bad decisions.

"Productive work is the central purpose of a rational man's life, the central value that integrates and determines the hierarchy of all his other values. Reason is the source, the precondition of his productive work. Pride is the result."

Rand proposes that we exist to accomplish something. Our purpose organizes and determines our priorities. Furthermore, if we get done the things that we were meant to do, we can and should be proud of our accomplishments.

"The smallest minority on earth is the individual. Those who deny individual rights cannot claim to be defenders of minorities."

I agree that individual rights must be upheld if any of the groups in society are going to have equal rights. Every group of every kind consists of two or more individuals.

"We are fast approaching the stage of the ultimate inversion: The stage where the government is free to do anything it pleases, while the citizens may act only by permission."

Rand died in 1982, but it seems that she was looking ahead several decades, much like Orwell did. She calls it the "ultimate inversion" because the people should be free, while the government should act only with the permission of the people, not the other way around, as it is in pure authoritarian dictatorships.

"You can avoid reality, but you cannot avoid the consequences of avoiding reality."

Sometimes its easier to just ignore your bills, the difficult work that needs doing, or the difficult conversation you need to have. That's fine for a few days or a few weeks, but eventually the consequences of reality will follow, one way or another. So rise up, acknowledge reality, face it, deal with the consequences, and look to the time beyond your troubles.

Ronald Reagan

Ronald Reagan appeared in 53 films from 1937 to 1964. He was the president of the Screen Actors Guild, governor of California, and then the 40th president of the United States during the 1980s. He was originally a Democrat lauded by Franklin Roosevelt and who supported Harry Truman. In the 1960s he switched to the Republican Party. In the 1984 presidential election he won 49 of 50 states. 1911 to 2004

"Government's view of the economy could be summed up in a few short phrases: If it moves, tax it. If it keeps moving, regulate it. And, if it stops moving, subsidize it."

Reagan believed that government meddling in the economy was detrimental to the success of the economy. Businesses should be allowed to succeed or fail on their own merit without help or hindrance from the government.

"We must reject the idea that every time a law's broken, society is guilty rather than the lawbreaker. It is time to restore the American precept that each individual is accountable for his actions."

I think it is clear that the world has been drifting away from the idea of personal responsibility, apparently for three or four decades at this point. I have been fortunate to know many successful people during my life, and I honestly never heard any of them blaming society for their mistakes. They tend to blame themselves for mistakes and then try not to repeat the mistakes.

"Government's first duty is to protect the people, not run their lives."

You may feel differently, but I agree with this idea. Everyone has a certain degree of freedom they expect and also a certain degree of security they desire. Sometimes the two aspects of life are in total opposition. To gain security means to give up freedom and vice versa.

"Trust, but verify."

Reagan really liked this saying, "Doveryai No Proveryai," which he borrowed from the Russians and used many times during negotiations. I used it myself often during my auditing career. It's funny when you think about it. I trust you, but just in case you're wrong for some reason, let's verify your numbers. If people want to take offense to your cautious approach, let them take offense.

"I know in my heart that man is good. That what is right will always eventually triumph. And, there's purpose and worth to each and every life."

This is engraved on the stone at Reagan's gravesite in California. Though there certainly has been plenty of wrong in the world, thank God that right does eventually triumph.

"The best minds are not in government. If any were, business would steal them away."

He was honest about a problem that has been growing for decades. The president's salary is $400,000 a year today. CEOs, CFOs, sales people, small business owners, tech executives, doctors, insurance brokers, and a host of other folks can and often do make more than that. Why would these hard driving smart people enter an industry where the second highest position in the whole organization (Vice President) makes $235,000 a year? The most talented young people are normally looking for more compensation than that.

"Concentrated power has always been the enemy of liberty."

Power and control go hand in hand. Someone who is completely free is uncontrollable by definition. Hence, concentrated power and control over people means less liberty for a population. I don't know how important your freedom is to you, but I know my liberty is sacred to me.

"Freedom is never more than one generation away from extinction. We didn't pass it to our children in the bloodstream. It must be fought for, protected, and handed on for them to do the same."

In human history freedom is the exception, not the rule. If America takes a careless approach to maintaining its freedom, some tyrant will gladly come along and impose his will and control. That control always starts small and ends up as total control if left unchecked.

Jean Paul Richter
German romantic writer, who was born 1763 and died 1825.

"Men, like bullets, go farthest when they are smoothest."

You have probably met some prickly and thorny individuals along the way in your life. In my opinion, it is much harder, though not impossible, for them to succeed in life. I agree with Richter's assessment that it's easier to rise in this world with a smooth demeanor. If rising is something you want to do, dress well, be polite, speak correctly, look your best, speak well of others, and try not to offend. In other words, be smooth.

Tony Robbins
Prolific American motivational speaker, author, and television personality. Born 1960.

"When you are grateful, fear disappears and abundance appears."

I firmly believe that gratitude is one of the keys to finding happiness and contentment in your life. Start your prayers, (if you pray) with the many things to be thankful for, before asking for the things you lack.

"The power of positive thinking is the ability to generate a feeling of certainty in yourself when nothing in the environment supports you."

Finding a way to believe in yourself when it seems that no one else believes in you is a key to overcoming adversity and living your best life. You cannot always rely on an external system of support. Sometimes there is only you, and you have to be the one who builds the fire that keeps you warm.

"Your past does not equal your future."

This is a great message that many around the world could benefit from. Your past certainly affects you, but it does not have to define you. A troubled past can turn into a bountiful future and vice versa. You can change your life to a tremendous degree in just a few months if you decide to.

"It is in your moments of decision that your destiny is shaped."

Don't make important decisions carelessly. Take all the time you need. Some of your decisions have serious, long-lasting consequences. Seek all the guidance you have time to seek and look at the situation from every angle. Then make a decision, and run with it.

"The only people without problems are those in cemeteries."

And, heck, as much as we understand about the universe, they may have problems, too. The point is: don't walk around thinking you are the only one with problems.

Everyone you know and everyone you see has problems as well.

"One reason so few of us achieve what we truly want is that we never direct our focus. We never concentrate our power. Most people dabble their way through life, never deciding to master anything in particular."

One of my business partners was very likely the best auditor in the state of Missouri. I hired him and watched him work for 20 years. What set him apart and made him literally twice as productive as everyone else was FOCUS. He has the ability to run at a high level of intensity for hour after hour, day after day, without letting any distractions affect the quality and quantity of his work. Time and time again I have noticed that the highly focused surgeons, dentists, or electricians were the ones making the most money for the longest time, due to the reputations they built. They were not making huge money because they were coming at the world with excess greed; it was rather that the world was coming after them for their excess talent and skill.

"No matter how many mistakes you make or how slow you progress, you are still way ahead of everyone who isn't trying."

Years ago we needed a new HVAC system at one of our offices. I asked four contractors to give us a bid. Two of them did not show up. One of them showed up and then never gave us a price for the project. This left the one, out of four, who bothered to show up and present a price. He got the job, of course. The scenario struck me and made me wonder how often in this world someone wins the day by merely showing up and showing the slightest bit of interest. It's probably a much bigger percentage than we would expect.

<u>John D. Rockefeller</u>
He was the founder of the Standard Oil Company and the world's first billionaire. However, he was more than just a 19th century capitalist. He was a problem solver and thought a great deal about the meaning and purpose of life. 1839 to 1937

"The secret to success is to do the common things uncommonly well."

> I think his point here is that there is not some special magic to building success. It is a series of doing a bunch of normal things better than most people do them. It is paying attention to the details and getting all of them right.

"You should rather hire a man with enthusiasm than a man who knows everything."

> This idea of hiring for enthusiasm, rather than for experience, is something that Southwest Airlines was famous for in the early days of its rapid expansion. I've done this myself a few times while hiring in a few different capacities. If I ran across people who were particularly great with customer satisfaction, I tried to hire them if at all possible. Their current knowledge was unimportant because they could learn the details of the new job later. They were already good at making customers happy.

"If you want to succeed, you should strike out on new paths, rather than travel the worn paths of accepted success."

> I view this statement a couple of different ways. First, you should avoid letting anyone else (or society at large) define success for you. The only success that will be fulfilling is the kind that you personally seek. Secondly, Rockefeller may be saying that the worn paths are crowded and full of competition. Find another new creative path to success without anyone in the way.

"Go as far as you can see. When you get there, you'll be able to see further."

I have not heard this much, but I love it. This is how you
achieve something that other people think is impossible.
You set out towards a goal, not knowing the whole path
ahead, and the further you get down the path, the closer you
get to the obstacles in the way, and the easier it becomes to
see the way over or around them.

**"A man's wealth must be determined by the relation of his
desires and expenditures to his income. If he feels rich on
ten dollars and has everything else he desires, he really is
rich."**

This is hard to understand in our modern social-media
consumption-based system, but there is a lot of wisdom
here. This is especially interesting coming from the world's
first billionaire. You would think he would say you need
great wealth to achieve great happiness, but instead he said
that spending less than you make and having everything
you want is good enough to qualify as "rich." Think about
the man who loves to hunt and fish and build log cabins.
He could be pretty happy in Alaska with very little money.

**"When work goes out of style, we may expect to see
civilization totter and fall."**

Are we on our way there? It seems to me that people aren't
working as hard as they once did. Maybe we are working
smarter or maybe we are working less and heading towards
decline. Time will tell.

**"Singleness of purpose is one of the chief essentials for
success in life no matter what may be one's aim."**

This is one of the most important tenets in this book. I
have seen this common trait in those who achieve great
things: exceptional focus on one purpose. The people who
do awesome things do not get distracted easily. They have
a single mission (at least for a period of time), and they
pursue that mission relentlessly as the primary focus of
their energy.

"The road to happiness lies in two simple principles. Find what it is that interests you and that you can do well, and when you find it, put your whole soul into it with every bit of energy and ambition and natural ability you have."

Rockefeller spells out a recipe for success and happiness here as clearly as can be. I will say that it isn't always easy to find that thing that we can stay focused on and that we can do well, but I absolutely agree that we should try. If and when we find that purpose, we need to give it our all.

"The way to make money is to buy when blood is running in the streets."

This is a different way to state Warren Buffet's rule about being greedy when people are fearful. It isn't easy to buy when everyone else is selling, but it certainly is the time to get a good deal if you have a long-term time horizon.

"I believe that love is the greatest thing in the world, that it alone will triumph over might."

Now, I will bet that is something you did not expect to hear from John D. Rockefeller. I hope he is correct. If love does not triumph over evil in the long run, we're all done.

Will Rogers
Popular American humorist, actor, and author. 1879 to 1935

"Good judgement comes from experience... and a lot of that comes from bad judgement."

This one is near the top of my list. It is a reconfiguration of a similar quote by Mark Twain. Try to remember it the next time you make a mistake and you think you got nothing but pain out of it. You actually learned what not to do, which could be even more valuable. The more you learn about what not to do, the closer you get to excellence. I think this quote is especially good to share with young people, who are out there trying new things, trusting the wrong people, and making mistakes that they, hopefully, will not make again.

"I don't know why people believe in God, but thank God they do."

This one is touchy and complex. Is there a god? Did God make man, or did man make God? I think Will's point is that maybe it doesn't matter. To Rogers, it is not plainly evident why people have faith, but it's super-important to society that they do. For some people, their belief in God is the only thing keeping them from going off the deep end. For a small contingency, a belief in God may be the only thing stopping them from uncontrolled pillaging and plundering.

"The platform will always be the same, promise everything, deliver nothing."

Isn't that the ugly truth about politics? When I think back about everything I have heard politicians promise and everything I have subsequently seen them deliver, 99% of it never happens. Worse yet, they often know in advance that they cannot deliver what they're promising. Somehow voters have short memories though and keep re-electing politicians that do not deliver. However, we cannot blame the voters entirely. With the current cost of getting elected and the current salaries of senators and representatives, the voters often don't even have a candidate on the ballot with a proven record of integrity and real-world success.

"Even if you're on the right track, you'll get run over if you just sit there."

Rogers's point is that it's not good enough to just get yourself on the right path; you have to move down it as well. Let's say you find yourself with a scholarship to a great university. If you don't go to class and don't do the work, you'll be out of that great university in short order – a lot of potential but no results.

"You can't legislate intelligence and common sense into people."

It's kind of funny when you watch citizens and politicians call for one more law to fix the problem that the last 100 laws did not fix. We cannot have one police officer and one judge for each free citizen in this country. To a certain degree, we need an intelligent and logical citizenry in order to function. What if 1/3 of the people casually drove on the left side of the street? What if 1/3 of the populace walked into stores and walked out with whatever they wanted without paying? No number of laws would fix the chaos.

Eleanor Roosevelt
Niece of Theodore Roosevelt and wife of Franklin Roosevelt. First lady from 1933 until 1945 and U.S. delegate to the United Nations from 1945 to 1952. 1884 to 1962

"Great minds discuss ideas; average minds discuss events; small minds discuss people."

I heard this quote on the radio many years ago, and thought to myself, "Yes, absolutely." People spend too much time gossiping about the petty actions of other people. Sometimes it's just about celebrities that they'll never meet, who have no actual impact on their lives. Let's spend more of our precious time discussing the important things for our families, our descendents, and our future – ideas.

"Nobody can make you feel inferior without your consent."

This is important to remember. Your self-worth is not determined by others, or at least it should not be. Others can attempt to make you feel stupid or worthless or inferior, but it's up to you to believe it or reject it. I spent many years with intense real-world pressure to feel inferior, but I fought the idea unceasingly the only place I could really win – within my mind. This same idea applies to the concept of embarrassment. No one can force you to feel it. When you have transcended the idea of embarrassment, you have sort of advanced to a higher plane of existence.

"The future belongs to those who believe in the beauty of their dreams."

We have to convince ourselves, and sometimes others, in the viability and value of our dreams and plans. Otherwise, we won't do what is necessary to pursue them.

Franklin D. Roosevelt
The only man who ever served more than two terms as president. The 32nd president was tasked with directing the federal government during the Great Depression and WWII – tremendous tasks. Franklin continued his early political career despite being paralyzed by illness in 1921. He become Governor of New York in 1929 and President of the United States in 1932. 1882 to 1945

"This generation of Americans has a rendezvous with destiny."

We now call them the "Greatest Generation", and they earned the title. They found themselves in a big economic hole after the Great Depression. Then they found themselves in a second world war to protect the freedom of humanity. They succeeded. Someday we may look back into history to rediscover the strength of our ancestors.

"Freedom of speech...Freedom of worship...Freedom from want...Freedom from fear."

These are some goals Roosevelt set out for America in 1941. The first two are protected in the Bill of Rights, and the last two were his aspirations.

"There are as many opinions as there are experts."

He was saying that back in the 1930s. How many more opinions and experts are there today? We are drowning in an ocean of information. Somewhere in the propaganda, lies, exaggerations, marketing, advertisements, and click-bait, there may still be experts with useful guidance, but finding it is now like finding the proverbial needle in a haystack. I actually revised that old saying a little. Now I say it is like finding the right needle in a needle-stack.

"If you treat people right, they will treat you right... ninety percent of the time."

I like sayings that are both humorous and poignant. This is his take on the golden rule, with the little 90% twist at the end. Treating people right is always the way to go. He is just pointing out that a small percentage of the population are just a-holes who are going to treat you worse than they should. Don't let them derail you from doing what is right and treating everyone with respect and courtesy.

"It is common sense to take a method and try it. If it fails, admit it frankly and try another. But above all, try something."

This sounds like the approach I took to marketing at the CPA firm. In a small business, you normally do not know what methods of marketing are going to be successful, but you do know that doing nothing will not work. So, you try and fail, try and fail, and just keeping trying new approaches until something works. This idea is useful in many aspects of life. You only reach true and permanent failure when you stop trying.

Theodore Roosevelt
One of the greatest presidents, protector of nature, and a devout adventurer. He was so popular in his time that he is one of the four presidents carved on Mt. Rushmore. 1858 to 1919

"It is not the critic who counts; not the man who points out how the strong man stumbles, or where the doer of deeds could have done them better. The credit belongs to the man who is actually in the arena, whose face is marred by dust and sweat and blood; who strives valiantly; who errs, who comes short again and again, because there is no effort without error and shortcoming; but who does actually strive to do the deeds; who knows great enthusiasms, the

great devotions; who spends himself in a worthy cause; who at the best knows in the end the triumph of high achievement, and who at the worst, if he fails, at least fails while daring greatly, so that his place shall never be with those cold and timid souls who neither know victory nor defeat."

Roosevelt reminds us that it's easy to talk about action or criticize those who take action, but the real and noble work is to take action and immerse yourself in it, regardless of the results.

"Believe you can, and you're halfway there."

I don't know if you are half-way there, but you certainly need to believe you can accomplish something just to begin the journey. Teddy was a man of great ambition and courage, who tried difficult things, such as starting a ranch in North Dakota at age 25. That didn't work out, but he started learning how to do hard things because he dared to try.

"The only man who never makes mistakes is the man who never does anything."

Roosevelt was undoubtedly a man of action and occasionally a man of mistakes. Trying new things generally involves some failure, so don't immediately judge someone a loser because they made a mistake. They may be a bold genius on their way to world-changing solutions, such as Thomas Edison.

"To educate a person in the mind but not in morals is to educate a menace to society."

This reminds me of how the prison system often fails. You take someone who was previously exposed to a handful of low-level criminals, and then have them spend several years chatting with hundreds of more sophisticated, more experienced criminals. They are also working out regularly and eating three balanced meals per day.

Without training in morals and ethics, what do you think happens when they get out?

"Knowing what's right doesn't mean much, unless you do what's right."

In the end, it is your actions that affect society a lot more than your intentions. There is an old saying, "The road to hell is paved with good intentions." Wanting to do good is fine, but you have to actually do good. Furthermore, I think we get more successful outcomes by rewarding successful actions rather than rewarding good intentions.

"Keep your eyes on the stars, and your feet on the ground."

I think he was saying go ahead and dream big, but don't spend so much time dreaming that you lose touch with reality. That's good advice. I'm a firm believer in pursuing big goals and also a firm believer in starting to pursue those goals right from where you are standing, with a firm grip on reality.

"If you could kick the person in the pants responsible for most of your trouble, you wouldn't sit for a month."

This is a clever, indirect way to tell you that you are the source of most of your troubles. It is human nature to blame anyone other than yourself, and the modern media makes it especially easy today. The hard truth is that generally we have made a bad decision, or a long series of bad decisions, that has led us into our troubles.

"In any moment of decision, the best thing you can do is the right thing. The worst thing you can do is nothing."

Roosevelt is encouraging us here to make a decision and run with it, preferably a correct decision. He sure does not like the passive notion of no decision and no action.

"Speak softly and carry a big stick; you will go far."

This is probably Teddy's most famous quote. The meaning is fairly obvious. Don't bully people, abuse them, or yell at them. Act like a civilized human being, but make sure people know you are a force to be reckoned with, not someone to be rolled over.

"I am an American; free born and free bred, where I acknowledge no man as my superior, except for his own worth, or as my inferior, except for his own demerit."

President Roosevelt held a firm understanding of equality. He viewed America as a land of equal opportunity but not necessarily equal outcomes. Americans are supposed to rise or fall by way of their own merits.

"A vote is like a rifle: its usefulness depends upon the character of the user."

A vote or a rifle could be used for good or evil. It all depends on the nature or character of the user. It would be great if we could ensure that only people of good character were using votes and guns, but that isn't feasible. For one thing, who will judge what "good character" is?

"The best executive is the one who has sense enough to pick good men to do what he wants done and self-restraint to keep from meddling with them while they do it."

The bigger the organization you are running, the less you will be able to follow the efforts of its staff. I only ran firms of fewer than 20 people, but I worked in companies with thousands of employees. I have certainly witnessed that great executives hire and foster excellent people and then give them the autonomy to do a great job.

"I am only an average man but, by George, I work harder at it than the average man."

This is a philosophy that I tried to instill in my children. You may not be smarter than all of the competitors.

That's okay. We can make up for it with hard work, and the whole family will do that hard work together, if necessary.

"The first requisite of a good citizen in this republic of ours is that he should be able and willing to pull his weight."

When I was managing people, it struck me that there were three kinds of team members: those who always helped pull the wagon, ones who sometimes pulled the wagon and sometimes rode in it, and occasionally some who strictly rode in the wagon. I encouraged the third group to go "work" somewhere else. For a business, group, or even a nation, I think it's useful to figure out who is working towards advancement and who is dead weight. Who is pulling the wagon, and who is just riding in it?

Giovanni Ruffini
Italian writer who lived 1807 to 1881.

"Rank and riches are chains of gold, but still chains."

Being held in golden handcuffs is not a problem that most people encounter, and many would scoff at the idea. However, if you know high-level executives, owners of multiple businesses, or professional athletes (or you are one), then you understand that one can be in a position of great income and great responsibility at the same time. Just because you make a lot of money does not mean you are free. There may be contracts to satisfy, people to manage, assets to manage, and debts to pay. Excess wealth makes it pretty easy to acquire so much stuff that the stuff owns you rather than the other way around.

Bertrand Russell
British philosopher, mathematician, logician, and author of Principia Mathematica. 1872 to 1970

"The fact that an opinion has been widely held is no evidence whatever that it is not utterly absurd."

Just to prove the point, here are a few examples: 1) At one time most people thought the Earth was flat and located at the center of the universe. 2) Not long ago, smoking was allowed on airplane flights, and almost no one complained about it. 3) Most of my life I was told that humans only use 10% of their brain. When I started personally running out of hard drive space (at about 45 years old), I realized that the 10% theory must be wrong. Old data had to go to make way for new. The point is that millions of people still believe and do a lot of crazy things. Don't let them peer pressure you into their delusions. Purchasing weekly lottery tickets is not a legitimate retirement plan; it's probably not going to work.

"The time you enjoy wasting is not wasted time."

This is something I need to remind myself regularly and more often. Many of us get stuck in a mode or a mindset in which production is good and lack of production is just bad. Obviously, life isn't all about production. We need to take time to rest and recharge, both physically and mentally, and we need to spend our precious time enjoying this beautiful life that we are living.

"Those who have never known the deep intimacy and the intense companionship of mutual love have missed the best thing that life has to give."

Our minds are built to think. Our bodies are built move. And, our hearts are built to love. To love someone and be loved by that someone surely must be the best thing that life has to offer. When I was younger, I would discuss with friends what it takes for a relationship to work. In your twenties and thirties you attend a lot of weddings, sometimes second and third ones. My assessment of the fundamental factor for a successful relationship was this: somehow both people have to feel lucky. That is the magic balance that fate must strike. Both people have to feel that they have someone who is better than they deserve.

Babe Ruth
George Herman Ruth was the first professional baseball player to hit 60 home runs in a season and one of the first five inductees into the Baseball Hall of Fame. 1895 to 1948

"Never let the fear of striking out keep you from playing the game."

I'm not a big baseball statistician, but I always remember that Ruth struck out a lot while he was hitting those 714 career homeruns. In fact, he led the American League in homeruns twelve times but also led the league five times in strikeouts. So, when you are at bat in life on whatever field that may be, and you occasionally strike out, just tell yourself, "It's OK; this is what happens to people who swing for the fences." Don't let that stop you from stepping back up and hitting a home run next time or the time after that.

George Santayana
He was a Spanish philosopher, essayist, poet, and novelist. 1863 to 1952

"Those who cannot remember the past are condemned to repeat it."

I feel that this is an important quote for society at large. There is so much to learn about humanity by studying history. We need to know the backstories of countries, cities, corporations, international relationships, wars, monuments, and a million other things. History helps us predict the unknown future and helps ground us in reality. In the last several years in America, we have been pulling down statues that teach us and remind us of our history. When that happens, we become more ignorant and more likely to repeat the mistakes of the past.

Jean-Paul Sartre
Twentieth century French philosopher, screenwriter, novelist, playwright, and biographer. 1905 to 1980

"The best work is not what is most difficult for you; it is what you do best."

It's common sense when you think about it. You and everyone around you is better off when each of you is doing the thing that you do best. Society is collectively the most productive. This philosophy starts to break down when you introduce the fact that people also want to enjoy their work, regardless of whether or not they're the best at it. Regardless, I do think it is a noble pursuit to find the thing that you do best and to make your living doing it.

"Only the guy who isn't rowing has time to rock the boat."

You could modernize it as, "Only the guy not working has time to protest." In fact, only the guy who isn't rowing or working has time to do anything elective or discretionary. I have pondered the sad reality that during much of human history, the masses did not have time to write, paint, study new scientific laws, master a musical instrument, or travel, because they spent all day every day growing and hunting food and maintaining a roof over their heads. We live in an opulent time now that allows almost anyone to pursue non-sustenance activities for over half of their waking hours. We should appreciate that blessing and make the best use of it, while we have it. We could be rowing non-stop.

"When the rich wage war, it's the poor who die."

You may have heard this one before. I recently looked up some net worth data and found that the median senator's net worth was around 20 times that of an active duty military family. One admirable thing about feudal lords was that sometimes when the king declared war, he led the charge into battle personally. It seems to me that's the way it should be. When you decide to risk the lives of hundreds of thousands of people, then put your own life at risk as well. Show us how it's done.

Johann Christoph Friedrich Von Schiller
Eighteenth century German philosopher, playwright, poet, and
historian. 1759 to 1805

"The voice of the majority is no proof of justice."

How many atrocities have been committed by the majority?
How many bad investments and crazy fads have the
majority pursued? How many innocent men and women
have been convicted in court, and how many guilty men
and women have walked free? This idea that the majority
must be right is an unfortunate glitch that I believe is
natural in the human brain – something we developed a
half-million years ago. If everyone around you started
running, you had better run, too. In modern times,
however, if you are not under fight-or-flight pressure and
have time to think about a situation, then right is right and
wrong is wrong. It doesn't matter how few people agree
with you on that. Stick to your own convictions.

**"Only those who have the patience to do simple things
perfectly will acquire the skill to do difficult things easily."**

To build mastery of a difficult skill, the path really is
learning and mastering a series of simple skills perfectly. It
certainly takes a lot of patience and a lot of time to learn
things like brain surgery, nuclear physics, violin, pole-
vaulting, or high-wire walking. Along the same lines, if
you want to be viewed as an expert in whatever field you
are in, don't forget to do the simple things well. If you
don't know how to use a copier correctly, people are going
to question your ability to dispense legal advice.

"Dare to be wrong and to Dream."

Dreaming is critical to our happiness, and I've discussed it
elsewhere. I want to address daring to be wrong. There is
so much fear today of being wrong. The world may record
a video of your incorrect action, post it on the internet, and

then possibly millions of people know that you were
wrong. So what! When you are a highly productive
person, you take a lot of action, and the odds of making a
mistake just keep going up. It will happen! When I was
running the firm, part of my role was to manage the fallout
from mistakes. This was the most successful approach I
found: 1) Apologize. 2) Tell the client that we strive for
perfection, but since we are human, we occasionally make
a mistake. 3) Find out what kind of solution the client
would like. 4) Focus on achieving that solution (if it is
feasible) as quickly as possible. To sum it up... Dare to be
wrong, and when it happens, admit it, and fix it. Then keep
the dream rolling forward.

Carl Schurz
German-American who served as a general in the civil war, a
senator from Missouri, and the Secretary of the Interior. Schurz
promoted the idea that government positions should be based
on merit rather than party connections. 1829 to 1906

**"You cannot subvert your neighbor's rights without
striking a dangerous blow at your own."**

These American civil rights that we have are for everyone,
not just for those who agree with you. If you deny some
basic rights to your neighbor today, you might find your
own rights being taken away tomorrow. I think this a good
reminder to Americans of today and a serious warning from
the past.

Arnold Schwarzenegger
A few years ago I read his autobiography. His journey was
really quite impressive.   A poor 15-year-old Austrian kid
decided that he was going to be a world champion bodybuilder,
and by sheer force of will, five years later he won Mr. Universe.
Then, without speaking English very well, he parlayed his size
and looks into a stunning American movie career that lasted for
decades. He even became the governor of California.
Born 1947.

Here is some of Arnold's excellent advice about how to succeed in life:

1. Don't worry about conformity.
2. Have a vision.
3. Trust yourself.
4. Break some rules.
5. Don't be afraid to fail.
6. Turn your liabilities into assets.
7. You'll never make the "impossible" possible without trying the impossible.
8. Never follow the crowd; go instead where they are not.
9. Aim straight for the top; everyone else is aiming for the bottom and the middle.
10. No matter what you do, selling is part of it.
11. Never miss an opportunity to meet and learn from a successful person.
12. Never let pride get in your way.
13. Don't over-think things; let the mind and the body float free sometimes, so that it's free to attack things with focus.
14. Forget Plan B. When you operate without a safety net, you are more likely to make Plan A work.
15. The day is 24 hours long; use them. Most people are not willing to work 12, 16, or 18 hours to achieve their goals.
16. Reps, reps, reps. Excellence comes from doing something over and over again.
17. Don't blame your parents. Whatever they did well or poorly, you will have to take care of your own problems from here on.
18. Take care of your body and your mind. Both can be trained and improved.
19. Stay hungry. Don't rest on your laurels.

Walter Scott
Scottish author, poet, and historian. You will find large monuments to him in both Glasgow and Edinburgh.
1771 to 1832

"To the timid and hesitating everything is impossible because it seems so."

Do you know someone like this? Everything seems impossible to them. It's one thing for them to park themselves on zero, but it's another to let them convince you not to pursue your dreams or that your dreams are impossible. Let your belief in yourself and what is possible live deep within your chest, as a flame that cannot be doused by anyone.

"What a tangled web we weave when first we practice to deceive."

Deception does indeed get overly complicated, and the consequences of being caught can be dire. Hence, just avoid it altogether if at all possible. Honesty is the best policy.

Seneca
Stoic philosopher of the first century, born in Spain and raised in Rome. ca. 4 BC to 65 AD

"It is not that we have so little time but that we lose so much."

At this stage of my life nothing frustrates me more than wasting my time. The older you get, the more you realize the value of time. So many people these days spend so much of their time on unimportant activities. I'm guilty, too. For example, how many thousands of hours of my life have I spent watching television that did not need to be watched? Hard to say. But, we can't go back in time and recoup the wasted parts. We can only move forward wiser and with a better sense of how to spend our precious time.

"A well-governed appetite is a great part of liberty."

Seneca is not just talking about an appetite for food; he is talking about all of the various appetites that one might have: drinking, sex, drugs, adrenaline, smoking, spending, etc. I believe he is saying that if you can control your appetites, rather than the other way around, it goes a long way towards giving you freedom. It allows for mental, physical, emotional, and economic freedom, as opposed to servitude to some addiction.

Dr. Seuss
Theodor Seuss Geisel was a prolific American children's author and cartoonist, selling over 600 million books. 1904 to 1991

"Be who you are and say what you feel because those who mind don't matter and those who matter don't mind."

Let's be straight and truthful with one another. If you have to pretend to be someone else to be in a relationship, you don't need that relationship. This goes for employment relationships, personal relationships, and all other relationships. Be yourself and share how you feel, and let the chips fall where they may.

"Why fit in when you were born to stand out?"

Amazingly, each and every one of us is different. Some of us were born to pull the wagon, drive the wagon, load the wagon, or build the wagon. Some will even stand on a ball and juggle while riding in the wagon. C'est la vie. If you were born to stand out, then stand out – pay the price or reap the rewards. If you were born to fit it, then relax, fall in line, and fit in.

"The more that you read, the more things you will know. The more that you learn, the more places you'll go"

Another self-evident quote but an excellent message for children and young adults. It's really not a bad message for all of us, at any age. Keep reading, keep learning, and keep going new places.

William Shakespeare
Quite simply the most famous and important playwright in history. He was also a poet and actor. 1564 to 1616

"It is not in the stars to hold our destiny, but in ourselves."

To Shakespeare our destiny is not all about chance and fate, but rather it is up to us to shape our destiny.

"Be not afraid of greatness. Some are born great, some achieve greatness, and others have greatness thrust upon them."

We should not be afraid of greatness in ourselves, our family, or our associates. Furthermore, we may not be born great or achieve greatness through effort, but we never know what circumstances may thrust greatness upon us sometime down the road.

"We know what we are but not what we may be."

It is true that we remember where we came from, and we hopefully understand where we are on life's journey, but no one knows the future. No one knows the true potential within us, not even ourselves. This makes life difficult and exciting.

"Words are easy, like the wind; faithful friends are hard to find."

Words certainly were easy for William Shakespeare considering that he used over 20,000 words in his plays and poems, and amazingly, he is credited with creating over 1,700 words that did not previously exist in the English language! Apparently, he learned that good and faithful friends were much harder to find than words. I don't know what your experience is, but my perception is that we will only meet 10 or 20 potential friends in our lifetimes with whom we connect at the highest level. Notice when that happens, and hang on to those precious lifetime friends as hard as you can.

George Bernard Shaw
Irish playwright and winner of the Nobel Prize in Literature.
1856 to 1950

"Life isn't about finding yourself. Life is about creating yourself."

I like this idea of our destiny not being set in stone. Yes, we should figure out who we are and what our purpose is. However, if we don't like who we are, there is a chance to change it. There is a possibility of becoming something better.

"A government which robs Peter to pay Paul can always depend on the support of Paul."

This is meant to be something of a joke, but it's also true. Governments are always out there choosing winners and losers, sometimes even creating winners and losers directly by way of grants, contracts, taxes, persecutions, and penalties. You can think it's wrong all you like, or you can accept it as a harsh reality and use it to your advantage.

"When we know what God is, we shall be gods ourselves."

He may very well be right about this. I'm suspicious of anyone who is sure that they understand the true nature of God. It's a pretty arrogant stance if you think about it. Can a worm understand what a human is?

"We don't stop playing because we grow old; we grow old because we stop playing."

There isn't much we can do to stop our bodies from eventually deteriorating with age, but we certainly can keep our minds sharper and happier by continuing to play and have as much fun as possible all the way to the end.

"I learned long ago, never to wrestle with a pig. You get dirty, and besides, the pig likes it."

It's funny, but there is a point here, as well. Try not to fight on someone else's terms. If you have ever watched mixed martial arts fighting, you have noticed that some people want to box, some want to grapple, some want to kick, and some want to stay on the ground. If you are smart, you will fight in the way you choose and not on someone else's terms. Utilize your advantages, and I'm talking about battles of all sorts: work, legal, relationship, consumer, and beyond.

"Some men see things as they are, and say why. I dream of things that never were, and say why not."

The people in the first half of this statement are doing better than the majority. At least they see reality and question why it operates as it does. The people in the second half are the builders. Those are the people I like to be around – the ones who can dream of a new reality and make it happen.

"Youth is wasted on the young."

I remember feeling immortal and indestructible. Life plays a mental trick on us when we are young. We perceive time as almost infinite. Even one school day sitting in a desk seems like it will be an eternity before 3:00pm, when school lets out. We have boundless energy to play all day, and we can be awed and inspired by so much. Physical beauty is effortless. Then things gradually take a turn south. That perception of time just keeps spinning up faster and faster as we age, and of course our energy declines and sense of awe, as well. We work harder and harder to maintain strength and flexibility. Nothing is as easy as it used to be. Maybe not everyone does this, but I think a lot of older folks see the young and inside their own heads say, "You have no idea what you have." So kids, to the best of your ability, start appreciating that youth and making the most of it. It actually doesn't last forever.

William James Sidis
Sidis was believed to have an IQ in excess of 250. If correct, that would make him the smartest man in recorded history.
1898 to 1944

"The universe is infinite and eternal."

He may have figured out a hundred years ago what
scientists might verify a hundred years from now.
We'll see.

Socrates
Is there a more well-known philosopher in history than
Socrates? He lived from about 470 BC to 399 BC and is
considered to be one of the founders of western philosophy.
When I discuss other "ancient" Greek or Roman philosophers,
note that some of them were teaching 500 years after Socrates.

**"Employ your time by improving yourself in other men's
writings, so that you shall gain easily what others have
labored hard for."**

> This is similar to the idea of learning not only from your
> mistakes but also from the mistakes of others. Today we
> might translate it as "Be open to read and learn from
> anyone else's ideas because the alternate is to learn all the
> lessons yourself the hard way."

"Let him that would move the world first move himself."

> This reminds me of the well-known saying, "Be the change
> you wish to see in the world." Simply, if you want to
> convince others of the effectiveness of a policy you intend
> to present to the world, first follow it yourself and show the
> way. I want to hear investment advice from a self-made
> millionaire and longevity advice from someone who looks
> 20 years younger than they are. Don't you?

**"True wisdom comes to each of us when we realize how
little we understand about life, ourselves, and the world
around us."**

> We indeed need to humble ourselves in order to be open to
> true wisdom. I like to say that we are never as smart as we
> are at 18 years old. It may not be exactly 18 for everyone,
> but there seems to be a point at which you think you have it

all figured out, and then you spend the rest of your life correcting that notion. When one of my daughters was 18, she told me that she knew more than I did at that point because I had been out of high school for so long. There was no point in arguing with her. I had a good laugh inside my head.

<u>King Solomon</u>
According to the Bible, he was the wisest man on earth at the time who reigned over Israel for decades during the 900s BC.

"Words kill, words give life; they're either poison or fruit; You choose."

Words are cheap and easy to say, and yet somehow incredibly powerful. Folks running for president have nothing really to offer, except words. The same thing goes for televangelists, motivational speakers, and award winning writers. Again, they are offering us nothing but words, yet those words can mean millions in wealth, fame, and even control over others. Try to use those incredible words for good rather than to damage people.

"Your own soul is nourished when you are kind; it is destroyed when you are cruel."

I'm no expert on the condition of a soul. However, it seems correct that being cruel would diminish one's sense of self worth in the long-run, unless you are a psychopath.

"The man who walks with wise men becomes wise himself."

This just makes perfect sense. When you spend time with wise men and women, you see and hear a lot of wisdom. If your mind is open, in time you absorb and understand at least some of it.

"Under the Sun the race is not to the swift, nor the battle to the strong, nor bread to the wise, nor wealth to the intelligent, nor success to the skillful, but time and chance govern all. For man does not know his time."

You never know on any given day what time and chance have in store for you. Anyone may win and anyone may lose in a given situation, depending on the circumstances. This is a reason to become hopeful when you are hopeless and a reason not to get too heady when you are feeling invincible.

"Knowledge is of more value than gold."

You can certainly earn a lot of gold if you have the right knowledge today. Many of the great teachers throughout time have said that the best investment you can make is investing in your own knowledge and skills. With great knowledge and skills, you can lose everything due to bad luck or bad decisions and then make it all back again.

"What has been will be again, what has been done will be done again; there is nothing new under the sun."

I think Solomon is making the point that the problems people face have probably been faced before. Each of us has this small space in time and limited knowledge of history. It's easy to think we are facing a unique problem, which no one has ever had to solve before. It's probably not true. Study your history, and you might find the situation repeating over and over again. For example, look at the number of times nations have destroyed the value of their currency.

"As iron sharpens iron, so a friend sharpens a friend."

As I have mentioned elsewhere, a good friend will give you the constructive criticism that you need to hear. A good friend can compete with you on friendly terms – challenge you to run faster, jump higher, lift stronger, and think deeper. Find those types of friends and put the effort in to keep them.

"To gain riches is wise; to pay for riches with happiness is foolish."

Why gain riches, if you have to give up all of your happiness to get it? Happiness is the end goal, not the money. It's more important than a bank balance.

Sophocles
Very successful ancient Greek playwright who lived around 497 BC to 406 BC.

"Our happiness depends on wisdom all the way."

If he means the collective "our," as in society at large, the government needs wisdom to plan and execute good governance, and the electorate needs the wisdom to choose excellent leaders. Likewise, at the individual level, our chances for happiness increase when we plan and execute those plans wisely.

"One word frees us of all the weight and pain in life. That word is love."

Love certainly eases burdens and makes pain more bearable. A good parent is going to endure whatever hardship is necessary to help their children. A good spouse is going to overcome whatever struggles come their way in order to take care of their spouse. Love is the reason.

Barbra Streisand
Award-winning American singer and actress. Born 1942.

"Oh God, don't envy me. I have my own pains."

Recently, I spoke with a good friend about envy – about how it's toxic in a relationship. We discussed that a lot of the envy is misplaced anyway. If people knew the whole story, they wouldn't be envious. The next day he texted me this quote. It reminds us that rich and famous people are also subject to problems. The grass always looks greener on the other side of the fence, but it actually isn't.

Jonathan Swift
Irish author, satirist, poet, and Anglican cleric. 1667 to 1745

"Necessity is the mother of invention."

We have all heard this many times, right? Often times a
parent will tell their children this, especially when the item
they want isn't in the family budget. Really, it's a good idea
for anyone of any age to seek creative problem solving. If
you really need the thing, and it does not exist or is not
available, you will be driven to build it from scratch. And,
that might turn out quite well. While creating a solution for
yourself, you just may build a new solution for thousands
or millions of others.

"Vision is the art of seeing what is invisible to others."

Years ago, after getting involved with buying and selling
real estate, I noticed that most people could not envision.
They would see exactly what was in front of them without
envisioning how the situation might be improved.
Personally, I love taking charge of something and making it
better, and it doesn't matter what it is. I love visualizing a
thing in its best possible condition and then striving to get it
there.

**"When a true genius appears, you can know him by this
sign: that all the dunces are in confederacy against him."**

Have you ever been there? It's easy to think that you must
be the crazy one, but don't falter. Stand firm when the
dunces are aligned against you. Some time in the future
your genius and their stupidity will become apparent.

**"A wise man should have money in his head but not in his
heart."**

Note that this sentiment is coming from someone who was
once the dean of St. Patrick's Cathedral in Dublin. He
preached notoriously long sermons around once a month. I
think this religious man is saying that we need to be logical
and cognizant of money with our brains but not be in love
with money or the idea of being rich. This is a fine line
that can be hard to maintain for a lot of us.

"Blessed is he who expects nothing, for he shall never be disappointed."

This seems to me to be a solid strategy. Don't walk around expecting a bunch of money, favors, or some other kind of help from outside your family. Don't feel like you are entitled to anything. We are all born naked and alone, and we will ultimately die and end up pretty much the same way we started. If someone chooses to help you along the way, awesome. If they choose not to, oh well, that's what you normally get. Expect nothing, and be pleased when you occasionally get more than nothing.

"No man was ever so completely skilled in the conduct of life, as not to receive new information from age and experience."

Any wise older person that you know will tell you that they are still learning and intend to keep learning all the way until the end.

Publilius Syrus
Syrian playwright and philosopher who was originally brought to Roman Italy as a slave. 85 BC to 43 BC

"The rolling stone gathers no moss."

A nurse said this to me recently in reference to how to stay healthy as we age. This is a little different idea than the original author had in mind. His point was that people who are always moving, with no roots in one place or another, avoid responsibilities and cares. That's fine for those who wish to live the life of a traveler. However, I like the anti-aging take on it, too. We humans are meant to move. Talk to any doctor, and they will tell you that stagnation leads to death. At any age, to the best of our ability we need to keep stretching, walking, hiking, dancing, and keeping our mind in motion, as well.

"You can accomplish by kindness what you cannot by force."

There is a time for each action, right? We should always start with kindness and politeness and keep it there if at all possible. If kindness is not working, you escalate to basic civility, logic, and reason. If that isn't working, you might resort to the chain of command and go over someone's head. Force should be the last resort, reserved only for those who understand nothing but force.

"It is better to learn late than never."

The opportunity for redemption is always out there. You can make a mistake and make it again and again, but if you finally figure out your errors and the proper solutions, your future just got brighter. Never give up on learning and getting better.

"Never promise more than you can perform."

This is critical to maintaining integrity. If you go around promising things that you cannot deliver, it won't be long at all before no one trusts you. Then it becomes quite hard to operate in a community if you are known as a chronic disappointment or an outright liar. Better to under-promise and over-deliver. If you think you can accomplish something in three hours, tell them four. What do you think happens to your reputation in a community when everything you promise gets done even better and faster than expected? Infinite demand for your work.

"Prosperity makes friends, adversity tries them."

There is something within human nature that makes someone with money more attractive than someone without it, at least at a surface level. Many studies have proven it. Maybe people want to benefit from the wealthy person's generosity or see up close how they succeed. Maybe they feel more comfortable because they know the wealthier party doesn't need anything from them. Whatever the reason, prosperity makes more friends. On the flipside, adversity can try those friendships. Nobody wants to be drug into a problematic situation or be guilty by association. It's tiring listening to a negative or scarcity-based mindset. Be cognizant when communicating with friends that there is a limit to how much of your problems they want to deal with. You don't want to be overburdened with their problems, and they don't want to be overburdened by yours.

Rabindranath Tagore
Bengali philosopher, poet, author, painter, and Nobel Prize winner. 1861 to 1941

"I slept and dreamt that life was joy. I awoke and saw that life was service. I acted and behold, service was joy."

One of the best joys in life is to be of service to those who need it, but who really needs your help, how much service do they deserve, and what kind of service should they receive? These questions are up to you to answer. There is certainly no shortage of folks needing your help in the world today.

"You can't cross the sea merely by standing and staring at the water."

How many people try? You probably know some dreamers who never have and never will do anything but stare at the ocean. Encourage them, show them the way, and free their mind to take a chance. Your encouragement may make the difference to turn a dreamer into a doer.

"Let us not pray to be sheltered from dangers but to be fearless when facing them."

If you are going to live a full life outside of your house, you are going to face dangers sooner or later. If you can face those dangers with your eyes open, chin up, head on a swivel, and brain on high alert, you will tend to survive better. This idea of courage in the face of fear is one you will see repeatedly from many of the sages in history.

Terrance Tao
Award winning Australian-American mathematician and
professor at UCLA with a reported IQ well in excess of 200.
Born 1975.

**"Ultimately you should follow advice not because someone
tells you to, but because it was something that you already
knew you should be doing."**

> If some piece of advice or wisdom strikes a chord in you,
> that is a good sign that it's right for you. If you already
> suspected that you were headed down the wrong path and
> someone you trust confirms it, it's probably time to pursue
> a new path.

Mother Teresa
Well-known Albanian-Indian Catholic nun who founded the
Missionaries of Charity and was canonized as a saint.
1910 to 1997

**"People are unrealistic, illogical, and self-centered. Love
them anyway."**

> This is helpful to the world and also to your own happiness.
> If you can accept the fact that your family, friends, and
> acquaintances are less than perfect, you can stop feeling
> angry and disappointed every time they behave badly.
> Rather, try to find a sense of gratitude when they are
> surprisingly good. Also, realize that you are less than
> perfect and sometimes disappointing to your friends and
> family.

Nikola Tesla
Serbian-American inventor, engineer, and author. He was an
early, important figure in the study of alternating current and
wireless technology. 1856 to 1943

**"Our virtues and our failings are inseparable, like force and
matter. When they separate, man is no more"**

It is the nature of humans to be flawed. You must accept someone's flaws along with their virtues because there aren't any people available without flaws.

"All that was great in the past was ridiculed, condemned, combated, suppressed — only to emerge all the more powerfully, all the more triumphantly from the struggle."

As I have mentioned several times in this book, change is almost always suspected and rejected. New ideas are feared and assumed to be incorrect. However, great ideas, inventions, and policies eventually triumph in the end. It's just a matter of time.

"You may live to see man-made horrors beyond your comprehension."

Tesla did not live to see atomic bombs exploded or genocides after 1943. Let's all hope and pray that we don't see anything worse than what we have already seen.

"Most certainly, some planets are not inhabited, but others are, and among these there must exist life under all conditions and phases of development."

This seems like a logical conclusion to me, considering that the fundamental building blocks of life have been flying through space all over the universe for billions of years now. Life on other planets probably is, or was, or will be in the future.

Margaret Thatcher
First female prime minister of the United Kingdom and the longest serving one of the 20th century. 1925 to 2013

"Plan your work for today and every day, then work your plan."

I've always heard it in its simplified form, "Plan your work, then work your plan." But, I like it either way. In fact, I like it so much that I live it. I write in my planner what I intend to do each day, even weeks and months into the future. Then I do everything my planner tells me to each day if at all possible.

Henry David Thoreau
Important American author and naturalist philosopher.
1817 to 1862

"Any fool can make a rule, and any fool can mind it."

You can find all sorts of ordinances within cities and laws within states that make you scratch your head. My daughters, having inherited my DNA, take the approach of finding out the rules and then deciding whether or not they make sense, before blind compliance. Thoreau's thoughts on rules hold up today, just as well as they did in the mid-1800's.

"It takes two to speak the truth – one to speak and another to hear."

This idea is critical in human communication. No matter how true or salient your message is, you need someone who is open to hearing the truth, or else the communication is useless. There must be a basis for trust between individuals or else the message recipient isn't really listening. They may even be actively resisting the message. We have a lot of talking past each other going on en masse today and too much bad information coming from too many distrusted sources.

"You must live in the present, launch yourself on every wave, find your eternity in each moment. Fools stand on their island of opportunities and look toward another land. There is no other land; there is no other life but this."

We are each standing in a situation which has particular opportunities and risks, and that is the situation we must deal with. It is our starting point. Appreciate and pursue whatever opportunities are at hand because those are the only ones you have right now.

"How vain it is to sit down to write when you have not stood up to live."

As I have written previously, before we read or accept anyone's advice, we need to understand whether or not the advisor knows anything. Thoreau really wanted to understand the world and find truth before commenting about it.

"I learned this, at least, by my experiment; that if one advances confidently in the direction of his dreams, and endeavors to live the life which he has imagined, he will meet with a success unexpected in common hours."

By what I have seen in my life and the lives of my associates, I agree with him. If you have a vision and put the time in to make it happen, unexpected success will likely follow.

"Men have become the tools of their tools."

Apparently, we've been drifting that way for over a 150 years, since Thoreau died in 1862. It seems like the tools are taking over faster and faster and more thoroughly all the time. Imagine how we will maintain and serve the A.I. matrix in 50 years.

"Read the best books first, or you may not have a chance to read them all."

With millions of books out in the world, it is so hard to pick which ones to devote your precious time to. Maybe read the 25 most famous books in history or the 25 best selling books, for social reference if nothing else. I've met a lot of people who talk about books they have not read, such as the Bible, the Quran, the Vedas, or the Egyptian Book of the Dead. My advice is that you should not purport to know what is in any book unless you have read it. Take the time and read things for yourself, so that you are not misled by other people's errant interpretations.

Harry Truman
Senator from Missouri, Vice President, and the 33rd President
of the United States. At one time President Truman had the
nickname of "Give 'em Hell Harry." 1884 to 1972

**"I never did give anybody hell; I just told the truth, and
they think it was hell."**

> Apparently, there were some folks in the late 1940s who
> did not want to hear the truth. I would suspect that there
> are even more today. The lesson here is that you should
> not censor your delivery of the truth just because some
> people can't handle the truth. They need to get over it.

Donald Trump
He is the only man in history to become president of the United
States without being elected to any previous political position
or being a military officer. He is also only the second non-
consecutive US President in history. Born 1946.

"As long as you are going to be thinking anyway, think big."

> A simple concept, but why not? There are no rules on how
> big we are allowed to dream. Perhaps you could become
> president, too.

**"Sometimes your best investments are the ones you don't
make."**

> The point is that we should not pursue every investment
> that comes our way; some of them are bad. I've driven
> many miles, and flown some too, to look at properties that I
> did not buy. That's Okay. We don't normally ever consider
> the mistakes we almost made, but the impact is "huge," so
> to speak. Our mistakes can destroy our wealth, our career,
> our family, or even end our lives. Try not to make big
> mistakes, of course, but at least learn from them when they
> happen. Learn what not to do. You can even learn from
> the ones you almost made but, thankfully, did not.

"I try to learn from the past, but I plan for the future by focusing exclusively on the present. That's where the fun is."

Countless philosophers, from the Greeks onward, promote living in the present as a path to happiness and contentment.

"Remember, there's no such thing as an unrealistic goal – just unrealistic time frames."

I think the evidence supports that idea. Consider that over 99% of what humans have attempted to do has eventually been achieved.

"I like to think of the word FOCUS as Follow One Course Until Successful."

There isn't enough said or taught in the world about focusing, but I have indeed observed throughout my career that people who are the most focused get the most done and get paid the most. The lack of focus leads to a lack of productivity, mediocrity, or failure.

"Sometimes you have to toot your own horn because nobody else is going to do it."

I know tooting-your-own-horn is generally considered poor form and bad manners. However, I can tell you for sure that if you get beaten down far enough and feel sufficiently outnumbered, then you'll have no choice but to do this in order to survive mentally.

"In the end, you're measured not by how much you undertake but by what you finally accomplish."

This is an unpopular idea in the era of participation awards and the elimination of grades in grade schools. Does that philosophy lead to better results? Time will tell. In my own life, it seems that the real magic came from finishing goals and projects rather than from starting them.

<u>Lynne Truss</u>
English author, journalist, and radio broadcaster who wrote
Eats, Shoots & Leaves – a book about the proper use of
punctuation. Born 1955.

**"Proper punctuation is both the sign and the cause of clear
thinking."**

In this modern, fast-paced texting society attention to
punctuation seems to be faltering. Punctuation can and
does make a difference to the point of your message, and it
tends to reveal the depth of your education, as well as your
attention to detail. You and your close friends may not care
about how your written communication looks, but
somebody in your life and career will.

<u>Thomas Tusser</u>
Sixteenth century English poet and farmer. 1524 to 1580

"A fool and his money are soon parted."

This concept is playing out a billion times a day. How
many foolish expenditures have you made? I'm guilty, too.
My family tries hard not to spend foolishly, but it happens
sometimes. We are so aggressively marketed to today from
so many directions, it's hard to even stop and figure out
where all of the money is going, let alone take the time to
assess if a better deal is available or whether or not you
really need the item in the first place.

<u>Mark Twain</u>
This man deserves a large section of this book. He was the
author of the *Adventures of Tom Sawyer* and *Huckleberry Finn*.
He also toured the world for decades as a humorist and speaker.
Twain was an expert on disseminating wisdom who was right
up there with Benjamin Franklin in that respect. Here are many
insightful commentaries on life from the man legally known as
Samuel Langhorne Clemens. 1835 to 1910

"The most important days in your life are the day you are born and the day you find out why."

This drives home the idea that we all really need to figure out our purpose in life. There is nothing we can do to affect which day we are born or the circumstances into which we are born, but we can all certainly work on discovering our purpose for existing. We can all work towards living that purpose.

"Let us live so that when we come to die, even the undertaker will be sorry."

I suppose we could cheat by befriending the undertaker in advance, but the point is to become such a blessing to the world that everyone is sorry to see you go. Even the guy getting paid to handle your exit would rather have you alive than increase his revenue.

"If you tell the truth, you don't have to remember anything."

On the surface, this sounds like nonsense. However, what Twain was saying was that if you tell the truth, you won't have to remember any of the different lies you might tell to your associates. That could become quite complicated. If you always tell the truth, at least the way you understand it, everyone gets the same story. Easy.

"Keep away from people who try to belittle your ambitions. Small people always do that, but the really great make you feel like you, too, can become great."

The world could use a lot more of lifting each other up rather than tearing each other down. If you read books on success, you'll find that those who have risen to the top of organizations advise that you get ahead not by tearing down the people above you but rather by empowering and strengthening the people below you.

"Courage is resistance to fear, mastery of fear, not absence of fear."

This is a well-known quote from Twain, and there are many quotes on courage similar to it. The point is that courage is not walking around fearlessly. When you engage in a battle that you are sure you are going to win, is that courageous? Not really. Courage is rather fearing loss, yet engaging in the battle anyway despite your fear.

"Kindness is a language which the deaf can hear and the blind can see."

It seems to me that when I was growing up people placed a higher value on kindness. There was more helping each other. Parents kept on eye out to protect other people's children. Friends and family worked on each other's cars and houses with no expectation of payment or reciprocity. There was especially a difference in how kind people were to each other who happened to vote differently. Tip O'neill (Democratic Speaker of the House) would go the bar with Ronald Reagan and work out their differences over a beer. Some say they were even friends. In my mind, everyone you meet is worthy of your kindness unless they prove to you that they are not.

"All you need in this life is ignorance and confidence, then success is sure."

I think Twain's point is that if you knew all the troubles ahead that you would be facing, you would not be so confident. In fact, you probably would not start or would quickly give up and fail. In light of this, start marching ahead on your journey with ignorance and confidence. The ignorance and confidence will eventually turn into wisdom.

"The man who does not read has no advantage over the man who cannot read."

In other words, if you can read, you should read and improve yourself. For many years I have felt that "smartness" must be more than just the ability to learn. It must be the ability to learn, combined with experience and exposure to knowledge. A person with a 200 point IQ who has never read anything has limited knowledge. He could be smarter and more useful to society, but not until sufficient knowledge is plugged into that massive intellect.

"To get the full value of joy, you must have someone to divide it with."

For most people, if they lived alone on a deserted island with every material possession, that would be fun for a week or a month. However, soon it would be an empty and lonely existence, and they would trade most of those possessions for another person or two to share life with.

"Anger is an acid that can do more harm to the vessel in which it is stored than to anything on which it is poured."

You can hold your anger for decades, and it will just keep bothering you, maybe even destroy you. In the long-run, your retained anger is going to hurt you far more than the person who made you angry in the first place.

"Never argue with a fool. Onlookers may not be able to tell the difference."

It just looks like two fools arguing. You aren't going to change the mind of a fool no matter what case you present. Save your time and breath. Save your arguments for someone who will listen, and stay focused on issues that are truly important to your future and that of your family.

"It is easier to stay out than to get out."

Remember this before entering into any strange new situations, especially dangerous ones.

"Be careful about reading health books. You may die of a misprint."

Funny, but I think the more important point is that the health gurus change their stories about what you should and should not do every few years. At one time some doctors advised us to have a nice healthy cigarette to calm our nerves. They also used to cure mental illness in the 1950s with frontal lobotomies. I would counsel anyone to run any health advice through the filter of your own logic first.

"A person with a new idea is a crank until the idea succeeds."

This has been proven over and over again, but it is hard to retain faith in yourself and your vision when everyone around you is laughing. It's hard to maintain your faith in your sanity when everyone around is convinced you're nuts.

"Don't go around saying the world owes you a living. The world owes you nothing. It was here first."

This is a timely message for a lot of Americans today. We have lived through an era of entitlement and external support. However, the norm throughout history is that those who were not born into monarchies or aristocracies had to learn skills and apply them to survive. Rather than walking around thinking you are owed something from the world, I think it's healthier to accept that you will get what you get, and hopefully that is what you have earned.

"Sing like no one's listening, love like you've never been hurt, dance like nobody's watching, and live like its heaven on earth."

This is a beautiful piece of advice. We should all try it.

Mike Tyson
Mike Tyson is a talented and fierce boxer who had great success in his youth. When he turned 30 years old, his professional boxing record was 44 wins and 1 loss. He had some problems in his life, but no matter what happened to him,

he always kept moving forward. Personally, I have always enjoyed his sense of humor. Born 1966.

When Mike Tyson was asked by a reporter whether he was worried about Evander Holyfield and his fight plan, he answered:

"Everybody has a plan until they get punched in the mouth."

> I love this quote because it's direct and easy to understand. If you've ever been in a real fight, you know this is true. You get punched, and then you start reacting instead of thinking. It's true both literally and figuratively, for physical and mental fights. Sometimes you get into a fast moving argument, car accident, weather situation, or some other rapidly progressing problem. Don't be surprised when you respond in a totally unexpected way, perhaps a bad way. I know some of my knee-jerk reactions have been detrimental. Great solutions normally take some time to construct, so to the extent you can, try to anticipate problems and envision how you would respond to them if they came upon you suddenly.

Lao Tzu
Lao Tzu, also known as Laozi, was a Chinese philosopher who lived around 500 BC. He is generally regarded as the founder of Taoism.

"A journey of a thousand miles begins with a single step."

> I have repeated this to myself and others many times. I love the quote because it encourages us to get off our butts and start down a path. We can't always know how long the journey will be or where it will lead. Indeed, the number of steps towards a given goal may be incalculable, but every single journey starts with <u>one</u> step. Don't fear the journey. Just take the first step.

"He who controls others may be powerful, but he who has mastered himself is mightier still."

I think many of us spend our first 30 or more years learning self control. You aren't going to inspire a bunch of followers without it. It's almost a pre-requisite to enduring power and leadership.

"Being deeply loved by someone gives you strength, while loving someone deeply gives you courage."

This is very insightful, and I think it's absolutely true. I know whose love gave me great strength, and I know who I love that gives me courage.

"Give a man a fish and you feed him for a day. Teach him how to fish and you feed him for a lifetime."

I'm sure we have all heard this. Do we believe it and live it? It's hard to argue with the logic of the strategy, but it can be laborious to take the time and spend the effort to teach someone a new skill. In fact, they will need many skills to feed themselves for a lifetime. This is a lesson that the government, school systems, and a lot of non-profit organizations need to re-learn. Some of them find it easier to hand out fish than to train fishermen and fisherwomen. Society gains in the long run when more of us are productive and self-sufficient.

Sun Tzu
Chinese military general and strategist who is believed to have authored the famous book *The Art of War*.
circa 544 BC to 496 BC

"If you know the enemy and know yourself, you need not fear the result of a hundred battles.

It is indeed critical to correctly assess your strengths and weaknesses and those of the ones who attack you. And, if you have both of those assessments correct, you should know what the outcome of a battle will be. If you are certainly going to lose, then retreat and fight another day.

If you are certainly going to win, then why not try to convince your opponent to surrender?

"In war the victorious strategist only seeks battle after the victory has been won."

On the surface it doesn't make sense. How can you win the war before the battle? The answer is preparation. If you are vastly superior in every way before entering into battle, you have basically the war won before you begin it.

"The greatest victory is that which requires no battle."

I think the great leaders throughout time have understood this. War is a tragic and unfortunate reality that nations of the earth have endured too many times. It's better if you can achieve victory, or at least a negotiated peace, without bloodshed on either side.

"There is no instance of a nation benefitting from prolonged warfare."

Prolonged wars have indeed brought down many empires. In my opinion, they are not something we should pursue as a nation. They can be equally destructive in your own business and personal life. During my career, I witnessed that prolonged legal battles tend to be the most rewarding for lawyers, rather than for plaintiffs and defendants.

"A leader leads by example, not by force."

If you want to have true, loyal followers, then have them following out of a sense of respect, gratitude, and pride rather than following out of fear and oppression. The greatest leaders are out there sweating with their team and putting in more hours than anyone they lead.

Gore Vidal
American author and screenwriter. 1925 to 2012

"A good deed never goes unpunished."

You have probably heard this amusing quip, maybe even lived it a few times. You throw away some garbage, and then later someone says, "That was my stuff; I need it." You repair someone's broken bicycle for them, and they complain, "I wanted to fix that myself." I have been burned by my attempts at good deeds many times. It's frustrating, but all we can do is explain our good intentions to the "victims," unless we are going to dispense with good deeds altogether, which would be unfortunate for society.

"There is no human problem which could not be solved if people would simply do as I advise."

Funny, but also something to think about. We tend to have a bias towards solutions that we created. We tend to think that what is right for us must be good and right for everyone. When problem solving for others, we have to ditch that bias, and do our best to climb into someone else's situation, culture, income level, or age. A problem often looks different from another angle, and many times the solution changes based on someone else's perspective. If you want to know someone else's preferred solution, ask them.

Joe Vitale
American motivational author and speaker. Born in 1953.

"The universe likes speed. Don't delay. Don't second guess. Don't doubt. When the opportunity is there, when the impulse is there, when the intuitive nudge from within is there, act."

Reckless decisions can certainly lead you into bad situations, but I agree with this idea that when you see an opportunity, you need to move with the utmost speed. How many times have you found the great deal gone when you came back the next day, the job you wanted taken the day before you pursued it, or the house you wanted sold the

day before you tried to make an offer? You are in
competition with an awful lot of people for many things
you want in life. When you see an exceptional opportunity
for yourself, analyze it immediately, and seize it quickly.

Voltaire
Actually named Francois Marie Arouet. Popular French author,
philosopher, and historian. Voltaire was a contemporary of
Benjamin Franklin and an advocate for freedom of speech,
freedom of religion, and separation of church and state.
1694 to 1778

**"To learn who rules over you, simply find out who you are
not allowed to criticize."**

This is an interesting idea. Who actually controls your
speech? Is it your parents, spouse, employer, your school,
state government, federal government, or multiple entities?
There are darn few people in the world, at this point, who
can and will openly speak against anyone or anything. In
my younger years in the United States we were allowed to
criticize any individual or group, the state, or the federal
government without much concern about retribution. Not
so for the last several years. The efficiency of surveillance
and the "thought police" is amazing. Think for a moment
about who rules over you and whether they should.

**"It is dangerous to be right when the government is
wrong."**

How many political opponents have been jailed or exiled
throughout history? How many rebels and revolutionaries
have been tortured and killed? How many people who
knew too much about the powerful were taken out via
suicides and tragic accidents?

**"Our wretched species is so made that those who walk on
the well-trodden path always throw stones at those who are
showing a new road."**

This is another metaphor to illustrate a characteristic of human behavior – conform or be cast out. (Yes, I just borrowed a lyric from a Rush song.) People tend to believe that if everyone is doing it, it must be the right move. The few oddballs who are not walking the same path must be crazy, misguided, or wrong. Their divergence is so offensive to the conformists that they may even attack (throw stones at) the oddballs, who are blazing their own trail. Therefore, if you fancy the life of trailblazing, just be prepared for the incoming stones.

"Those who can make you believe absurdities can make you commit atrocities."

Voltaire said this around 1765. It is so insightful, almost clairvoyant, when you look at the wars and genocides that happened in the following 250 years. Never buy in to absurd ideas or atrocities, even if everyone around you is doing so.

"Common Sense is not so common."

Isn't that the truth? So many things that should be self-evident seem to escape a majority of the population. I'm not going to list them all, but here is one short example. Don't spend more than you make because you need to save something for the future. Simple, easy to understand, common sense. Yet, how many individuals are spending more than they make? How many businesses and even governmental entities are not following this basic common sense? We will all do well to foster our common sense and use it to manage our lives.

Johann Wolfgang Von Goethe
You could say he was Germany's version of Ben Franklin. He was a philosopher, poet, playwright, scientist, and statesman. 1749 to 1842

"Knowing is not enough; we must apply. Willing is not enough; we must do."

This quote makes me think of some of the accountants and bookkeepers that I audited over the years. You point out some errant balances, and the person responds, "I know exactly how to fix this; I just haven't done it yet." Well, that's fine, but the numbers are just as wrong as if you didn't know how to fix them. We need to keep ourselves and the people around us focused on results, not just knowing what to do or apologizing for procrastination.

"There are only two lasting bequests we can hope to give our children. One of these is roots, the other, wings."

I like his idea and the elegance with which he states it. We should give our children a stable foundation and solid family roots from which to grow. We need to be the tree that is not easily blown over. We can also give our children the education, resources, and encouragement to fly as high as possible.

"He is happiest, be he king or peasant, who finds peace in his home."

It is very stressful to be missing peace in your own home. Home should be your refuge from the chaos outside. If there is a way to do so, foster peace in your home for yourself and your family.

"Thinking is easy, acting is difficult, and to put one's thoughts into action is the most difficult thing in the world."

It's stated simply, but it's good to remind people that having a dream or a goal is really the easy part. Taking some action is harder, and probably the hardest thing to do is to orchestrate all of the necessary actions towards actually achieving one's goal. Sometimes that even means failing and starting over.

Kurt Vonnegut
Successful American author whose works spanned from 1952 to 2005. 1922 to 2007

"We are what we pretend to be."

This reminds me of the modern quotes: "Fake it until you make it" or "Perception is reality." In many professions, pretending to be the thing well enough and long enough will help you become the thing. I'll never forget what a business partner of mine said a few months after we bought the CPA firm. He said, "I don't know if you are actually an auditing expert, but you sure sound like one." My first thought after that phone call was, *Well, maybe sounding like one is all that really matters.* Over the course of about 20 years, I morphed from someone who sounded like an auditing expert into an actual auditing expert. If you care about your work and take pride in it, the world will probably give you a chance to become excellent at it.

George Washington
Heroic American general who became the first Commander-in-Chief of the Continental Army in 1775. He won the war with Britain by perseverance, discipline, and intense, masterful leadership. He became the first president of the newly formed United States of America in 1789.   1732 to 1799

"Few men have virtue to withstand the highest bidder."

Isn't that the truth still today? Washington was already wealthy before the revolution, and he risked literally everything to pursue the idea of freedom for his fellow citizens. How many politicians, lawyers, accountants, doctors, activists, and lobbyists sell their allegiance to the highest bidder today? How many people say the opposite of what they believe in exchange for dollars? Virtue includes saying what you really believe and doing what you know you should do, regardless of the outcome.

"Truth will ultimately prevail where there are pains to bring it to light."

As Washington implies, truth often lies in the darkness. When we work to bring it to light, it has the chance and power to prevail. I think that seeking the truth is one of the noblest causes we can pursue.

"It is far better to be alone than to be in bad company."

We certainly do need to choose our friends and associates carefully. How many people are sitting in jail today because of the bad company they were keeping? I can think of some situations where I carelessly chose bad company and regretted it. You probably can, too.

"To be prepared for war is one of the most effective means of preserving peace."

We call this idea of American foreign policy "peace through strength." It seems antithetical to keep peace by preparing for war, but it simply works in accordance with the laws of nature. Most animals do not attack things that look bigger and stronger than themselves, especially if they are indeed bigger and stronger.

Richard Whately
English philosopher, academic, and theologian. 1787 to 1863

"Lose an hour in the morning, and you will spend all day looking for it."

Funny. However, it is a good point that if you get your day started an hour late, you may be running behind all day. You'll certainly get an hour less of work done, provided you go to bed at the same time.

"It is the neglect of timely repair that makes rebuilding necessary."

You could apply this simple but true statement to many things: structures, land, relationships, bodies, institutions, and beyond. If you know me well, you know that I am always repairing and maintaining, to fight the degradation of my assets and myself.

"A man who gives his children habits of industry provides for them better than by giving them fortune."

A gifted fortune can be lost, and lost quickly, by people who did not make the sacrifices to earn it. However, enterprising productive young folks can go make a fortune, even if nothing is given to them or if they lose it all and have to start over.

Oscar Wilde
He was a renowned Irish poet and playwright, and you will find several statues of him in Ireland today. 1854 to 1900

"To live is the rarest thing in the world. Most people exist, that is all."

When he says "live," he means really live life to the fullest. It's a shame that many do not. I would gladly spend a thousand years doing new things, seeing new places, and fostering new friendships. How many people stay in the same place, doing the same activities over and over again until death?

"Be yourself; everyone else is already taken."

I always advise young people who are doing a lot of job interviews to be themselves in the interviews. If they pretend to be someone else, they will likely get a job that does not fit their personality. The job won't last long and will probably result in an unhappy employee and an unhappy employer.

"Conversation about the weather is the last refuge of the unimaginative."

I have always thought that a lot of conversations in the world are of little consequence, like chit chat about the weather. I understand that people like to keep it light. They don't want to reveal too much about themselves or hear too much about someone else. That's fine, but why not just move along and have a real conversation with someone you care about, or maybe even have a real conversation with someone you barely know? Maybe they are someone you should know, but if you stick to the weather, that deeper interaction is never going to happen.

"What is a cynic? A man who knows the price of everything and the value of nothing."

Do you know people who will buy nothing because in their minds no product and no experience is worth spending money on? I certainly have known some. In my opinion they are missing a big chunk of the joy to be had in life. Money is there not just to be piled up and looked at, but to be spent on travel, education, comfort, health, and solving whatever problems come our way. There is a balance, of course, to be maintained between spending nothing and spending yourself into bankruptcy. Keep spending everything today, and you will have nothing tomorrow. Keep waiting until tomorrow to spend, and eventually there will be no tomorrow.

"One of the many lessons that one learns in prison is that things are what they are and will be what they will be."

This idea that some things are simply out of our control is difficult for some people to accept. Living under someone else's control is a hard pill to swallow. By nature, we love freedom, or at least I do. We love to feel like we have everything in our lives under control, yet some philosophers believe that the best we ever have is the illusion of control. It's a nice illusion to live in, while you can. Of course, something always comes eventually and blows up your sense of control. That's life. Wilde's statement reminds me of the Serenity Prayer – the part about accepting the things you cannot change.

Marianne Williamson
American self-help author, speaker, and political candidate.
Born 1952.

"Our deepest fear is not that we are inadequate. Our deepest fear is that we are powerful beyond measure. It is our light, not our darkness that most frightens us. We ask ourselves, who am I to be brilliant, gorgeous, talented and fabulous? Actually, who are you not to be? You are a child of God. Your playing small doesn't serve the world. There's nothing enlightened about shrinking so that other people won't feel insecure around you. We were born to make manifest the glory of God that is within us. It's not just in some of us; it's in everyone. And as we let our own light shine, we unconsciously give other people permission to do the same. As we are liberated from our own fear, our presence automatically liberates others."

This quote was incorrectly attributed to Nelson Mandela for many years. The part that really stands out to me is that there is nothing enlightened about shrinking so that other people won't feel insecure. This happens all the time, doesn't it? People quietly sit at the back of the classroom, make no inquiries, and answer no questions out of fear of judgement. Their playing small doesn't help them or serve the world. Stand up, speak up, and rise to your place in the world.

"Joy is what happens to us when we allow ourselves to recognize how good things really are."

It's easy for a lot of folks (including myself) to keep focusing on what they do not have, what is broken, and what is wrong in the world, but if you want to actually feel joy, you have to flip the script and invert the situation. Recognize the many blessings, show some gratitude, and spend some time reveling in abundance.

Ludwig Wittgenstein
Austrian philosopher, author, and professor at the University of Cambridge. 1889 to 1951

"Whereof one cannot speak, thereof one must be silent."

This is just a little cryptic. He is saying, more eloquently, that if you don't know about a place or a subject, don't talk about the place or subject. If you don't know what you're talking about, there is no point to revealing your ignorance on the matter to everyone around you.

"The world is independent of my will."

I think he is saying that we can try all we want to will the world into compliance with our desires, but the world isn't going to yield. It does what it does regardless.

"A serious and good philosophical work could be written consisting entirely of jokes."

Probably true. I like when a lesson is both funny and true. You get to enjoy yourself and laugh a little bit while you're learning.

David T. Wolf
Twenty-first century American science fiction author.

"Idealism is what precedes experience; cynicism is what follows."

What Wolf has proposed here is a pretty normal progression. I'm thinking about several teachers that I've known who started teaching in inner-city schools to make a difference and then left within a year or two. It's quite easy to drift into cynicism when your ideal vision doesn't pan out. The key is to not stay in the cynicism, but rather to advance into realism. We need to see the world as it really is (to the best of our ability) and accomplish what is possible. If that works, and you still have extra energy, you might even take a shot at what appears to be impossible.

William Wordsworth
Well-known English romantic poet who lived 1770 to 1850.

"Life is divided into three terms – that which was, which is, and which will be. Let us learn from the past to profit by the present, and from the present, to live better in the future."

I like this idea of learning from the past to live better in the present and also learning here in the present to live better in the future. I think some people fall into a couple of traps. First, they had some problems in the past, and because the memories are painful, they don't want to ever think about those problems again or learn the lessons they teach. Second, because they get sufficiently comfortable in the present, they stop learning the new things that will be required to have a bright future. The key is to always be learning from the past and the present and building towards the future.

"Wisdom is oftentimes nearer when we stoop than when we soar."

This makes a lot of sense. When you are flying the highest, you neither have the time nor the humility to learn a lot of serious wisdom. On the flipside, when you are down and depressed, that's when you realize you aren't living right. Something serious needs to change. Now you're seeking new solutions, new answers, and new ways of being. As Stephen Covey said, "If we keep doing what we're doing, we're going to keep getting what we're getting." So, use those low times to learn some lessons and gain some lasting wisdom.

"The best portion of a good man's life is his little, nameless, unremembered acts of kindness and of love."

We hear about the university building named after some billionaire who gave $50 million or a local library funded by a rich widow. We normally don't hear about all of the beautiful little acts of kindness and generosity performed by the uncelebrated unknown heroes around you. No one knows when you buy a child's lunch because he forgot his lunch money, you paid to repair the leak in your car before selling it, or you drove some stranger to their home at 1am because it looked like they wouldn't make it. Hardly anyone knows when you bail a friend out of jail for a DUI or when you give your gym bag to a random teenager who liked the way it looks. However, all of the little things add up to a friendlier community that is more likely to pay it forward. Perhaps you'll need one of those little kindnesses, too, someday.

William Butler Yeats
Irish poet and writer who lived from 1865 to 1939.

"Think like a wise man, but communicate in the language of the people."

This approach was critical to my success as a CPA. Many clients, including doctors, lawyers, and engineers, thanked me for explaining the tax code in a way that was easy to understand. Whatever your job is, it is great to have a mastery of the jargon, laws, rules, and technical details, but you only reach the pinnacle when you can explain the most complicated concepts in terms that are easy for anyone to understand.

Frank Zappa
Creative American musician, composer, and band leader.
1940 to 1993

"Art is about making something out of nothing and selling it."

Personally, I love turning nothing into something. That is true creativity, in my opinion. I would not say that art isn't art unless it's sold, but it sure makes the artist happier to create art and then affirm that it is valued by an audience. Selling art also helps keep the artist alive and creating more art. Unfortunately, many artists throughout history haven't lived long enough to see their art valued, which is a shame.

Zig Ziglar
Well-known American motivational speaker and author.
1926 to 2012

"Gratitude is the healthiest of all human emotions. The more you express gratitude for what you have, the more likely you will have even more to express gratitude for."

I don't know exactly how the chain of events works, but I definitely believe he is correct. Maybe those people you express gratitude towards appreciate it and want to hear more of it. Hence, they help you again and again. Maybe something bigger and more complex is in play.

"You don't have to be great to start, but you have to start to be great."

Lao Tzu stressed the importance of taking the first step all the way back in the 5th century B.C. How many dreams have you had without taking the first steps towards achieving them? Hopefully, none, but if there are some, it's not too late to start. You never know where those steps might lead.

"The first step in solving a problem is to recognize that it does exist."

This is a simple idea, and it sounds self-evident. Surely, everyone can tell when they have a problem. Yet, how many people do you know who definitely have problems and definitely do not acknowledge them? Keep that in mind when someone goes out on a limb and tells you that you have a problem, there is a chance they're correct. At least listen with an open mind.

"There are no traffic jams on the extra mile."

You won't run into many people these days who serve you beyond your expectations. You won't see a lot of people doing more than they have to at work in order to be great at what they do. When you're going above and beyond, some naysayers will tell you, "You don't have do that; it's not your responsibility." Tell them this, "I know; I want to do it because this is how I do things."

Unknown

My apologies to whomever birthed these bits of wisdom. Some of them are attributable to multiple sources, and some sources are simply unknown. If I knew for sure whom to attribute them to, I would do so. They are great, nonetheless.

"We travel not to escape life, but for life not to escape us."

Travel has always been important to my family. There is so much to learn and experience by simply being there on the ground with the local residents, breathing their air, eating their food, drinking their drinks, observing their art, and learning their customs and philosophies.

"If you don't take care of your body, where will you live?"

I've had this thought myself. We all spend so much time taking care of our houses, cars, toys, tools, etc. Shouldn't we devote the biggest portion of our efforts to our own bodies? Like a lot of other folks, I'm guilty of excess stress, long hours, too much sugar, and insufficient aerobic exercise. We need to keep focused on the idea that our body is actually our primary residence and most valuable asset. It's not whatever building we happen to be residing in at the moment. If you are not healthy, you cannot take care of anyone else or any other assets.

"An easy dollar is hard to find."

Have you met someone who is always looking to make an easy dollar? I have found that most of those folks don't have a lot dollars. With the speed and ease of communication today, your competitors sop up those easy dollars pretty quickly. My advice is to take the rare easy dollars when they come, but be ready, willing, and able to work hard for most of your dollars. That's what it takes 99% of the time.

"Economists are people who work with numbers but who don't have the personality to be accountants."

After working with accountants for over 30 years, I would argue that economists are actually more outgoing and charismatic than accountants. At least you see them on TV or podcasts occasionally, sharing their forecasts. Regardless, the point I want to make is that everyone needs to pair their personality to a profession that is compatible. If you are 100% introverted, you will not be happy attempting to sell magazine subscriptions door-to-door. If you are 100% extroverted, you will not be happy sitting in a tiny, windowless corporate office writing journal entries all day.

"If you're already in a hole, stop digging."

This quote has been attributed to several different people and goes back at least 100 years. The author of the aphorism envisions a situation where you are stuck in a hole that you've dug, with no ladder to get yourself out. Figuratively, you have made some mistakes and find yourself in a bad situation. In these situations you need to stop and realize that whatever you've been doing is only making things worse, getting you deeper into a place you don't want to be. When you recognize that, you should consider a whole new strategy and maybe ask for help from wiser people than yourself. Maybe they have a rope and can pull you out.

"If you're gonna be stupid, you gotta be tough."

My good friend Phil was a prison guard for many years. He shared this prison saying with me long ago, and I have never forgotten it. It's a good reminder about negative consequences. When you are taking unnecessary risks and not paying attention to the realities around you, don't be surprised when bad things happen. Be vigilant, make smart decisions, and maybe you won't have to be quite as tough.

"Like all self-made men, he worships his creator."

Obviously whoever said this believes that all self-made men are conceited, too arrogant. When I think about the "self-made men" I have known, I don't think I would agree with this. Why? Because no one achieves great things without the confidence to at least begin the journey. Believing in yourself (confidence) is not the same thing as worshipping yourself. Just like there is a fine line between courage and stupidity, there is also a fine line between confidence and arrogance. Knowing what you might be capable of and trying to achieve it within legal and ethical boundaries is great. Believing you are entitled and invincible, and being willing to do anything to anyone to get what you want, is not greatness. That's a tyrant.

"After all is said and done, more is said than done." Also, **"Talk is cheap."**

I think you have all met the big talker, the person who goes on and on telling you exaggerated stories of goals and aspirations that will never be pursued. In Texas they say something like, "Big hat, no cattle." In other words, the guy wearing a giant expensive cowboy hat and talking like a big-time rancher probably has no cattle at all. Bottom line, you will do well in life to develop a keen radar for those who talk a lot and do very little. Don't believe anything they tell you, and do not act upon anything they suggest. Follow those folks that you know for sure are successes or have accomplished similar goals as to what you have in mind. Maybe you can learn something from them that will propel you in the right direction.

"The two hardest things to handle in life are failure and success."

When I think about the number of great actors and musicians who died too young from various addictions, I suppose great success must indeed be hard to handle. Most of us are more familiar with failure and get regular practice at handling that.

"Choose a job you love, and you will never have to work a day in your life."

This is a great aspiration and a saying that we have probably all heard. In reality I think it's hard to achieve and maintain. Some folks start out loving an activity, and when it becomes their sole source of sustenance and a serious responsibility, it loses some appeal. Hats off to anyone who is loving their profession day in a day out. You have won the lottery without having to buy a ticket. For the rest of us, a career that feeds us in multiple ways and keeps us mentally and physically healthy has to be good enough.

"When motivation fails, discipline prevails."

My friend Ron repeated this quote to me recently. He is a successful YouTube video producer of the channel known as Ron's Basement. On the surface, the quote doesn't make sense. However, if you think deeper about it, you realize there is a difference between motivation and discipline. Motivation is more fleeting, like excitement about a new project or a temporary diet. Discipline is more permanent. It is the way you are living every day – a commitment that you will not break or stray from. When you get to the gym and don't really feel like working out but do it anyway, that's discipline.

"If it weren't for the last minute, nothing would get done."

It is true that some people work towards deadlines. We saw this every tax season. A small portion of our clients would wait until the last couple of days of tax season and then dump off their documents on us. Those are the procrastinators, and I found that their behavior rarely changed. The more important take away from this quote is that we all need a deadline of some sort. We need to set a time limit for accomplishing a goal. Otherwise, it can just be pushed endlessly out into the future. Without a deadline, a dream would probably remain just a dream.

"If you need something done, find the busiest man in town."

The saying may have started with Ben Franklin, but I have
definitely heard it said by my uncle Jimmy. I love this
quote because it's counterintuitive and also true. People
tend to give work to those who have nothing to do, but
that's kind of like going to a restaurant that has no
customers. When you see that one restaurant has three
customers and another one across the street has 50, there is
probably a good reason for the imbalance. Save yourself
some time and trouble. Find the company with all the
customers because they deliver the speed, quality, and price
that everyone is looking for.

"Pigs get fat, and hogs get slaughtered."

I first heard this saying in the late 1990s, but it goes back at
least 100 years before that. It is typically used in business
and finance to express the idea that it's okay to make some
profit, but if you get abusive with your prices, you'll be
taken out. You'll lose customers, get sued, or be undercut
by competitors. Rather than doing that, if you will just be
reasonable with customers, you will have all of them that
you can handle. This idea can be transferred over to a lot
of areas in one's life. Enjoying a little excess in life once in
a while is fine, but if we make a habit of drinking, eating,
or partying to great excess, then disaster is coming sooner
or later.

"When the going gets tough, the tough get going."

Have you known truly tough people, people who will do
whatever it takes to protect their friends and family? Have
you known people who recognize when hard work is
required and then pick up their tools and start doing it?
These are the people you want on your team, the friends
and family you can count on in good times and bad. Life is
too difficult and precarious to align yourself with those
who run in the other direction when the going gets tough.

"Money can't buy happiness."

Well, yes and no. When I was in college, I remember a psych professor discussing happiness and money based on psychological studies. At the bottom end of the income scale, more happiness certainly does correlate with more money. Think about someone in poverty, making $15,000 a year. Another $15,000 would be quite helpful to them. However, for someone making $1,000,000 a year, another $15,000 may mean nothing at all to their happiness. That said, you can certainly be happy with close to nothing or miserable as a billionaire, depending on the rest of the circumstances in your life – health, relationships, friends, age, physical danger, legal peril, etc.

"Under-promise and over-deliver."

This is a commonly used mantra in the business management world. It simply means that customers will be happier if you commit to less than you think you can deliver and then deliver more than they expect. It makes perfect sense, yet in the last many years we have witnessed a whole lot of over-promising and under-delivering on the customer service front. The good news is that it's becoming easier and easier to stand out if you are the source of exceptional customer service.

"Hope is not a strategy."

This is something I heard for the first time recently, and it immediately struck a chord with me. Hope is not a strategy; it's just a desire for something to happen. How many times have you heard someone say, "I'm hoping to get a new job" or "I'm hoping to get out of debt." Well, that's fine, but what practical actions are you taking to make it happen? Maybe spend 5% of your time hoping and 95% of it working towards the object of your desire.

"It is easier to get forgiveness than permission."

This is known as Stewart's Law of Retroaction. I think it is better used as an occasional strategy than a way of living. Yet, I have met several people in my life who do it non-stop. These are the sort of people who dump a pile of trees on your property or park their camper on it and then wait to see if you say anything about it. They are bullies, and some of them have gotten away with it so long that they expect impunity everywhere they go. It works, until the unstoppable force meets an immovable object. Then what? Explosion and destruction. My point is that, after assessing the threats, opportunities, risks, and rewards, if you want to boldly go forth with an unapproved action, do it. However, don't make a habit of it, unless you want to spend your life in trouble and in non-stop battles.

"If you're not a rebel by the age of 20, you've got no heart; if you're not establishment by 30, you've got no brains."

This idea has been stated in different ways by different authors during the last 150 years. I first heard it in the movie *Swimming with Sharks*. I immediately had an "aha" moment. This is mostly because I was quite rebellious towards authority by 20 and fairly assimilated into the establishment by 30. Evolving and changing is natural – many people do it. I realized in my thirties that the best way to improve a system is to work within the system. Outside of the system there is no money, no power, and no influence.

"If at first you don't succeed, you're about average."

This is meant to be funny, but it's also true. There is a pervasive myth in the world that those who succeed have done it on their first try. That is occasionally correct, but more often than not there is an unpublicized record of struggle and failure that eventually led to success. Is someone a failure when 99 times they tried something that did not work, or are they a success because on the 100th try they found the correct solution? Bottom line, do not condemn others, or yourself, for trying and failing.

"All things are temporary."

This idea has been espoused by many philosophers going back at least 2,500 years. It's best to remind yourself of the temporary condition of all things when you are living through trouble or suffering. Whatever the trouble is, it is temporary, and you can take heart in that. On the other hand, it's a sad reminder that when you are flying high and winning repeatedly, the good times are also temporary. Right after you set a record or a personal best of some kind, the very next condition is less than the best. You are now getting worse rather than better. So be it. That's life. Our strength ebbs and flows, our skills peak and decline, and eventually our temporary life is over, too.

"If there is anything better than to be loved, it is loving."

I feel like this quote should carry on a little to clarify and finish with "the people who love you". When I read it the first time, I thought *but what about the folks who are loving someone who does not love them back?* You have probably seen that sad situation somewhere. Being in love with someone who does not love you is an unfortunate state of affairs, but to have love flowing in a two-way direction, that is glorious.

"It is in our nature to seek the infinite."

Look at the way man is always seeking to go further and faster, to learn more and more about everything. It's clear that, as a species, we are never content. This includes both spatial infinity and spiritual infinity. Some think that the first religions go back as much as 70,000 years. This human need to understand our place in time must be deep-seated.

"The odds of being born are 1 in 400 trillion."

The actual odds are probably even slimmer, like winning the lottery a million times. We walk around every day thinking about our lack of this, that, and the other thing, without appreciating the incredible miracle that WE were ever born. I think we need to remember this frequently and remind ourselves and each other about our biggest and most fundamental blessing. We are sentient animated beings who have somehow beaten incredible odds and come into existence. Congratulations!!

Proverbs

In researching quotes for this book, I came across several "proverbs" of unknown authorship attributable to certain areas of the world.

"Trust in Allah, but tie up your camel."
Arabian proverb

In other words, have faith in God that everything will work out fine, but also take some responsibility to ensure a favorable outcome.

"He who sacrifices his conscience to ambition burns a picture to obtain the ashes."
Chinese proverb

If you let your ambition cause you to act in opposition to your conscience, you will lose all self-respect. You will have lost something precious and received something basically worthless in return.

"Hope for the best but prepare for the worst."
English proverb

I like this idea. It keeps you moving forward but not without a plan for the possibility of failure. People who know me well think my outlook and worldview is too negative. My natural approach is: outwardly expecting the worst, while inwardly hoping for the best. I don't recommend it. The English proverb path will probably make you a more likeable individual. From a charisma standpoint, it's probably better to publicly hope for the best, while you privately prepare for the worst.

"He who pays the piper calls the tune."
English proverb

This has been around for some centuries. In the modern era we like to say, "Follow the money." There is also the cynic's alternative to *the Golden Rule*: "He who has the gold makes the rules." Have we not seen this story play out over and over again, especially in the justice system in the last few decades, starting with the OJ Simpson verdict? There seems to be one set of rules for those who are the most politically connected and those who can fund the best attorneys indefinitely and another set of rules for the rest of us. The moral of this story: either pay close attention to he who is paying the piper, or become the piper payer.

"First secure an independent income, then practice virtue."
Greek proverb

If you study the lives of early scientists, artists, and philosophers, you will find that many of them were born into money, married into money, or were supported by a wealthy family. When I was younger, I used to think about this sad issue of not being able to pursue higher-level activities due to want of sustenance. How many great men and women in history were boxed out of achieving their highest purpose because they spent nearly every day of their lives securing basic food, water, and housing for themselves and their families? How many good people did bad things because they felt they had to in order to survive? The ancient Greeks already understood the conundrum. If you want to be virtuous, one of the first things you are going to have to do is secure an income stream - one way or another.

"It is better to be a coward for a minute than dead for the rest of your life."
Irish Proverb

> This is an interesting idea. I would give it a conditional thumbs up. Generally, you should not let your ego get in the way of your survival. However, I can think of a few scenarios where the duck and run strategy is a no go. For instance, I would fight to the death to protect my wife and daughters and not regret it.

"Doveryai, no proveryai"
Russian proverb

> This is translated as, "Trust, but verify." It was one of Ronald Reagan's favorite sayings, and I like it a lot. It's a good reminder to both have some faith in people and also maintain some skepticism. If you get push-back from business associates, friends, or salespeople when you verify what they are saying, just tell them that any human could be wrong about something for a variety of reasons. Admit that you have occasionally been wrong, as well. I have given out incorrect information with great confidence several times, and I'll bet you have, too.

"Be happy while you're living, for you're a long time dead."
Scottish Proverb

> Don't we get hung up on too many unimportant annoyances and forget to be happy? I know I do. I want you and I to sense the urgency of finding and feeling happiness in this very plane of existence, for we're a long time dead.

Quotes from Shawn Williamson
No, I haven't deemed myself one of the great philosophers. However, I have had some ideas that I arrived at without borrowing them from others, and you can judge their usefulness for yourself.

Life is a balancing act between short-term and long-term happiness.

You can have it all today and nothing tomorrow; nothing today and everything tomorrow; or something today, tomorrow, and every day for the rest of your life. Let me explain. If you run wild seeking everything you ever wanted immediately today, you may end up in jail or dead by the end of the day. If you deny yourself every pleasure in life long enough, you may end up dying before you get to enjoy your life. The goal should be to find a balance that maximizes your happiness across your lifetime. Plan your future with the rest of your life in mind, but don't forget to also enjoy today because tomorrow may never come.

Sometimes smart people make bad decisions.

It took me until around 40 years old to thoroughly realize this concept. The natural assumption is that smart people make good decisions every time. Well, the reality is they don't. So many things can get in the way of good decisions besides intelligence: lack of experience, lack of information, time pressure, family expectations, gluttony, sloth, and the other seven deadly sins. Hence, don't trust anyone's decision automatically. Vet it first with your own logic, and perhaps bounce it off multiple wise associates.

You can rise to power in three ways: by birthright, by tyranny, or by charisma.

Since the birthright path is unavailable to most people, and the path of tyranny is rather unpleasant, most people will choose the path of charisma. Sometimes the path to power may involve a combination of the three.

If you don't like what you see in the mirror, take a couple of steps back.

It's kind of a joke, but it works both literally and figuratively. We tend to get overly absorbed in our flaws and pay too much attention to them. Do they really matter to your family, friends, or the rest of the world? Probably not. Give yourself a break. Back up from the mirror and judge the whole you, not each tiny flawed part.

Most great achievements require setting up and knocking down a long series of dominoes.

This is another way to say that you achieve a large goal by accomplishing many small goals in the correct order. A seemingly impossible goal looks a lot more possible when you break it down into the smallest components. It is similar to the old joke: How do you eat an elephant? One bite at a time. Start chewing.

The world loves a specialist.

After looking at thousands of tax returns, I noticed that the people who made over a million dollars a year tended to be specialists: orthodontists, heart surgeons, personal injury attorneys, designers of unique tech or bio-tech products, or salespeople for niche computer services. Generalists make a lot less. Why? The world is just not impressed by someone who can do 20 different things with average competence. The market is willing to pay the most to get the best. It's that simple. If money is one of your objectives, whatever you do, be the best at it. Honestly, even if money is not your objective, when you are the best, the money will follow you automatically.

Anything that you think you know just might be wrong.

One day in 1988 I learned that the name that I used for almost 18 years wasn't my original name, and my parents weren't really my biological parents. You probably will never hear something that shocking, so here is a more mild example. One time I had a huge argument with another CPA firm over an accounting rule that I was sure I knew. Well, to sum it up, I didn't. You probably have your own story about something you were sure of that turned out to be wrong. If you do not yet, you will. My advice is to always maintain a bit of uncertainty about all things. If you fight to defend a falsehood, it becomes embarrassing and not helpful to you or anyone else.

If you know someone you wish to be your friend, first sincerely care about him or her, before you expect that person to sincerely care about you.

I think people can tell when someone takes a sincere interest in their well-being versus a shallow interest for a self-serving purpose (like selling you a product or service). The easiest way to appear to have a sincere interest in the well-being of another individual is to actually care about that individual. It's short-sighted human behavior to think *What's in it for me from this relationship?* The better approach is to consider *What can I do for the other party in this relationship?* Maybe they will appreciate it and maybe they won't, but generally people want to feel respected, valuable, and supported. Think about how you can bring that to the relationship.

If you don't have charisma, at least act like you do.

As you have seen by now, this is similar to my favorite types of quotes – somewhat funny but also carrying a serious message. I am a firm believer in the power of charisma. A tiny minority of folks have natural-born charisma. Everyone likes them, follows them, and wants to be their friend or business associate. They are destined to succeed in almost any endeavor that involves sales. For the rest of us, all is not lost. We can learn what charisma looks like and study the aspects of it, and we can work on improving our own.

If you are willing to do the things that no one else is willing to do, that's when you get paid.

I used to say this a lot years ago when I was growing the firm. Recently, a good friend of mine repeated it back to me, which proves he was listening many years ago. This is a concept that I noticed from observing the income streams of tax clients over the years. The ones doing activities that no one else wanted to do were normally quite well paid and in demand. It's not the only way to make a lot of money, but it's one way.

Moving through life is like driving down a highway with nothing but the rearview mirror.

What is ahead is always a mystery, like a completely opaque front windshield. It's annoying, at least to me, to not be able to see the future clearly. All we can do is keep looking at the recent past and extrapolate what is most likely ahead. Maybe the straight, smooth road behind us is also ahead of us, or maybe a curvy, rough road is ahead.

Every failure gets you closer to success, if you pay attention and don't give up.

It's easy to give up after a failure or two. However, if you keep paying attention to why you fail, then you can eliminate incorrect strategies. One day, after some number of attempts, you just may find the correct path to success, provided that you never give up.

It's smart to learn from your mistakes and even smarter to learn from someone else's.

While growing up, I paid a lot of attention to what did not work for my relatives, friends, and other associates. I figured if something did not work for them, it probably would not work for me either. I certainly made some mistakes, too, along the way and learned from them. If you and I ever get together for a chat, I would be glad to tell you about my mistakes, so you can avoid them.

Free your mind to dream, and free your hands to build the dream.

It's easy to let peers and authority figures cage your mind by telling you all of the things you can't do. Sometimes they even control your body by keeping you in a classroom or sitting at cubicle. I have always rejected the limitations foisted upon me, and I encourage you to do the same. Run free towards whatever dream compels you.

Grateful Acknowledgements

I want to thank my wife, Dawn DeEtte Williamson, for her excellent proof-reading skills, editing, command of the English language, and tolerance of me.

I want to thank my friend, editor, and fellow author, Anthony Clark, for his effort, experience, and guidance. Also, thank you to my friend Steve Boyer-Edwards for his help with graphics and proofreading. If you are a friend who has given me an important quote or suggested an important guru to be included in this book, I thank you, as well.

Lastly, after reading this book, if you have found that there is useful knowledge within it and have decided to share it with others, then I thank you for that.

About the Author

I would like to at least briefly give you a rough outline of who I am, my education, and the important experiences that shaped my worldview.

I am the child of two young people who knew each other a short time in Greenville, North Carolina. I was adopted at a few days old by my great-great uncle and grew up in two places: a giant trailer park north of Chicago, called Park City, and a small town in southern Illinois, called Flora.

Despite being in trouble fairly often in grades K through 12, I graduated as the valedictorian of Flora High School in 1988. Thankfully, I received several college scholarships, which were critical to my ability to attend college. I worked hard, made a lot of friends, and received a B.S. in Accountancy from the University of Illinois with High Honors.

After working as an auditor at a large CPA firm in Chicago, Crowe LLP, I moved to the St. Louis area and worked as an auditor at Enterprise Rent-A-Car and then at a couple of local CPA firms. While working and helping care for a toddler, I went back to school at Southern Illinois University Edwardsville, where I received my Masters in Business Administration. While in school there, I worked for the SIUE Foundation, supervising the undergraduate students who called on the alumni for donations.

Upon graduation, I was hired as the president of a local property management company, managing about 400 units and a team of property managers and maintenance men. After firing and hiring the whole staff once or twice, and getting my hands quite dirty, I dragged a business that was losing $10K/month to profitability in about nine months. Let's call that experience a PhD from the School of Hard Knocks.

After the property management game and with a second baby on the way, I got serious. In November 1999 I took a job at a local CPA firm again, this time with a plan to buy half of it. On January 1, 2001, I bought half of the firm and changed its name to Fick, Eggemeyer & Williamson, CPAs. In the years ahead, we served over 3,500 clients, providing bookkeeping, payroll, income tax preparation, business consulting, and auditing services all over Missouri, Illinois, and the rest of the country. During my tenure, I helped lead the firm to 21 years in a row of record revenue and tremendous profit growth, which improved my life a great deal. I retired on January 1, 2022, handing the firm over to about 20 people that I helped hire and train. I trusted them with the firm and still trust them today to succeed in perpetuity.

My writing career started in 2007 with a book of poetry (of all things) called *Slipping In and Out of the Light*. That was something I had been slowly compiling for about 20 years. In 2010, I finished Part I of my Autobiography, called *Headed Towards Infinity*. In 2013, I published a book called *Big Success in Small Business, Lessons Learned from a Thousand Small Businesses*.

Big Success in Small Business had a bit of success, which was great fun. Those who read it really enjoyed it, and some even bought multiple copies to distribute to their entrepreneurial friends and business associates.

In 2016, I started writing monthly articles for Successful Farming Magazine and Agriculture.com. During my tenure as a contract writer for Meredith Corporation, I had 75 articles published on a broad range of finance, legal, tax, and general business topics with the final one coming out in the December 2022 edition of the magazine. The story I wrote in 2017 on the high cost to start up a new farming operation was the most read story of the year for the magazine.

Post CPA-firm retirement, I worked for Buckingham Strategic Wealth for about a year as a senior tax manager and penned a few tax and finance articles for their website and financial advisors. The last year and a half of my accounting career I worked for a Washington-based CPA firm as a tax consultant, advising several hundred clients of Fisher Investments.

Starting in my teens and throughout my business career I've invested in many different mediums: precious metals, stocks, bonds, mutual funds, ETFs, options, promissory notes, and residential, commercial, and agricultural real estate. I'm a firm believer in the time value of money, compounding, and capitalism.

In my family life, I have been happily married for over 30 years now to a wonderful partner and friend, Dawn Williamson. She is my proofreader, editor, and a critical judge of a thousand crazy ideas. We have enjoyed visiting over 30 countries together. I also have two great daughters, Madeline and Grace, who are well on their way to success and happiness in their own lives.

Made in the USA
Monee, IL
22 September 2025